WAITING FOR DRAKE

www.waitingfordrake.com

WAITING FOR DRAKE

Fears, Hopes, Interests and Obsessions

Adam Wayne

www.waitingfordrake.com

Published by; WFD Publishing.

P.O.Box 657, Rochester, Kent, ME1 9HT

ISBN 978-0-9569816-0-8

My thanks to Steve for his help with the cover art. Thanks also to Jimmy for his valued opinions regarding the text of this work.

A catalogue record for this book is available from the British Library.

Printed and bound by MPG Biddles.

DEDICATION

For my daughters, that they may have a future.

Drake he's in his hammock till the great Armadas come,
(Capten, art tha sleepin' there below?),
Slung atween the round shot, listenin' for the drum,
An' dreamin' arl the time o' Plymouth Hoe.
Call him on the deep sea, call him up the Sound,
Call him when ye sail to meet the foe;
Where the old trade's plyin' an' the old flag flyin',
They shall find him, ware an' wakin', as they found him long ago.

CONTENTS

PREFACE

Dear Mark,

This is not an encyclopaedia. It is not a reference book. It is not a highly researched political tome. If it is read at all, it will be dismissed as the ranting of a mad, delusional dinosaur who cannot accept the world the way it is.

It has no index, nor does it contain footnotes. There are no laboriously gathered statistics, I am sick of reading statistics that contradict that which is blindingly bloody obvious to me.

It is an unashamedly self indulgent work. It is not an attempt to persuade or cajole, I have largely given that up. It is more an expression of exasperation at the lunacy that surrounds me. It is a troubled walk though my disbelief and a view of England through the bewildered eyes of one who cannot believe what the hell we have allowed to happen to us. If you require the technical, systematic destruction of all that ails us then sadly, you will have to look elsewhere. This is simply a personal view. My little book is written by myself and for myself, and for anyone who shares my incredulity. Its purpose is simply to commit to record my own frustrations and fears.

I do believe that things in England could change but I do not believe that they will. This is not an auspicious way to begin I admit but this is, after all, an attempt to highlight the truth. We may as well start as we mean to go on.

I resort to humour at times but this is more a nervous default than an intentional methodology. It is, in any case, humour of the gallows variety and certainly of a pretty low form. The book is a mixture of musing and scribble, points that have occurred to me at certain times and which have circulated my mind awaiting this effort. It will win no prizes but I am in the happy position of being beyond caring what people think and am ambivalent about its reception. I imagine that my scribblings are an attempt at catharsis, a wild gambit to purge my inner self in the hope if not the expectation that this may cheer me up in some indefinable and most unlikely way.

I have looked at many of the differing issues that plague us but found, not to my complete surprise, that a great many (if not all of them) have their roots in our apparent need to exterminate ourselves as an identifiable entity. Thus, as all roads led to Rome, it would appear that our troubles stem from a desire to replace ourselves as you might do with an old car or a faulty kettle. Inevitably therefore, the book became largely concerned with our nations declining numbers and with the underlying causes of this decline.

I have touched on the prickliest of prickly issues of our day, some of which are hardly touched upon at all anymore. I do not expect even you (the most right minded and intelligent of beings) to agree with all that I vent. Then again, if everybody agreed with me on everything then I wouldn't have anything to moan about. I do however hope to land the odd telling blow.

I do not have a politically correct bone in my body. This is very liberating, you should try it. Political correctness does not exist to change the character of a people; it exists in order to silence them whilst they are being destroyed. No one should ever be able to tell you what words you can use. There is no point in PC language as it so corrupts what you have to say that it becomes barely worth saying, if at all. You can't have a decent conversation if you have had half of your vocabulary stripped out and consigned to the memory hole.

It is a convention that any argument, feeling or principle that is, or could ever be perceived as being 'right wing' must always be qualified by a preamble such as, '*I am not sexist but.*' As this is extremely boring I will simply declare a universal qualification for everything that follows and just let you read the book.

I would be sorry if anybody took genuine offence at anything I have written but I am very comfortable that the sensitivities of others are of less consequence than my right to speak my mind.

The PC Nazis will consider this book to be disgusting. I sincerely hope so. I would quite like them to feel some of the disgust that correspondingly I feel for them.

Adam.

Kent

Spring 2011

But the sea wife's child bearing is about done. The stock is running out, and the planet is filling up. The wives of her sons may carry on the breed but her work is past. The erstwhile men of England are now the men of Australia, of Africa, of America. England has sent forth 'the best she breeds' for so long, and has destroyed those that remained so fiercely, that little remains for her to do but to sit down through the long nights and gaze at royalty on the wall.

Jack London 1903

ONE

WHY?

A nation which has forgotten its past can have no future.

Sir Winston Churchill

I was finally driven to this by seeing a clip on the telly of Nick Clegg telling of how hard his little job is and how it makes him cry that that people don't like him anymore. Although his sobbing drew some sympathy from the public; I confess that I wanted to insert an 'I agree with Nick' placard somewhere that really would bring a tear to his eye. Of all the things that could have set me off you may consider this a strange one but actually I suppose that it is as good a reason as any, he is an irritating little toad.

As I begin, I stare out of the window at the garden shed that I have spent all day painting the wrong shade. It is very dark (the shed that is), a little like my mood and I have missed a bit round the side, a job for next year perhaps. It is quite symbolic (well it is a *little* symbolic) of the state of play in Old England. We have put in so much work but the end result is unsatisfactory. We haven't paid enough attention; we have been distracted by drinking tea and listening to the radio. There is something wrong but we do not wish to address it now, maybe later. We need a recoat but it is all too much effort

I work in the City as a stockbroker. It is a taxing and infuriating profession, less a science and more of a black art although it used to be quite good fun until the regulators took hold and decreed that we should all be earnestly miserable. I was once a barman amongst other things which was much more entertaining. Not in the City mind you but in the East End where I, fag in mouth, dispensed wisdom, sympathy, light and bitter and cheese toasties with panache. I liked it. You got to drink for nothing and chat to women that you ordinarily wouldn't have dared to. If the guvnor was out it was even better. I would sometimes mistakenly give the impression that *I* was the guvnor (to said women) and would drink a lot more (for nothing). I especially enjoyed being able to refuse to serve beer in pint glasses to the militant feminists that came in from the alleged university down the road. The fury! I loved that. Two halves each and that's it. Great stuff.

It was fascinating to hear the conversations in what was essentially a 'boozer'. I learned much about human nature which incidentally has stood me in pretty good stead in my later occupation. I also learned a million dirty jokes which sadly have no place here. I hail from a very large and long established East End family and so the wide boys amongst the clientele would feel comfortable enough to tell their little stories to my great amusement and education. I would also listen to the working men railing against the injustices of the world and the locale in particular. Some of these men were very, very articulate. Some were as thick as mud but all deserved a hearing, their betters certainly weren't listening. Such fury and bitterness I would hear. All the more astonishing then that these men couldn't bring themselves to do anything to address their situation and continued to place their faith in people that had no interest in or feeling for them. By the time that the locals had 'sussed out' their friends in the Labour Party as the treasonous, treacherous dogs they are, the locals were in such a minority they could have all voted ten times each and still not prevented the red Quislings from keeping the keys to the borough.

I hate the modern Labour Party. It has no discernable redeeming qualities and the abandonment of its core vote is one of the great betrayals of our history and there have been a few. I exaggerate not when I say that is an internationalist, self serving force for evil and its leaders are our mortal enemies. They may even be those lizard things that David

6

Icke keeps banging on about. My detestation of Labour will be a recurring theme throughout this work; I hope you won't tire of it.

When I was behind the bar watching my home town disappear, I comforted myself with the belief that things may turn around when the English people came to their senses. They didn't. They still haven't. They are still drinking tea and staring at royalty on the wall.

The East End is an excellent place for us to begin as in my lifetime it has been changed beyond all recognition. This is not a physical change in terms of streets and buildings and all that sort of thing, much of the place is as it was when I was a child. The change, as you well know, is in the population itself. It's about time somebody said this, so here goes.

The Englishmen of East London have been largely ethnically cleansed.

They have been ejected and flung out to all points Kent and Essex, a veritable cockney Diaspora if you will. Some people went of their own accord, or at least they thought they did. Some departed quoting a yen for the countryside (Dagenham and Basildon). Some will tell you that they sought a gentler pace of life (commuting up and down the A13).

Then again, some will tell you that they did not wish their children to attend schools that 'spoke' dozens of different and impenetrable languages. Some will tell you that they couldn't bear the oppressive, frightening atmosphere that engulfed their home town once immigration really took hold. Some will tell you that they wished to live amongst their own people. These people have had their tongues cut out and this book is for them.

I am often homesick. It is a peculiarly wrenching kind of sickness like the longing for a lost lover who will never return. It saddens me when others speak of returning home for my home no longer exists outside the memories of those that dwelt there. My family lived in East London for centuries and I could count my relations in the many hundreds. Virtually all have now left to escape the new paradise bestowed upon us. There are a handful of pubs where the stranded congregate, a smattering of the marooned or stoically defiant but not many. A cockney brogue in the streets comes as a surprise amongst the deafening roar of alien faces and speech. It is a tragedy yes, but more so a sin, an act of vicious vandalism wrought by the weak and the wicked.

Are we meant to celebrate this awful disaster? We are certainly instructed that we should do so and any dissent is still ruthlessly purged by the Nazi liberals and socialists. How should we celebrate? Maybe in a crack den or a high rise tower block, in the urine stained lift perhaps? Perchance we should enter into the spirit of and acknowledge the purpose of the exercise and just murder ourselves; we are certainly not welcome anymore. The salt of the earth to the scum of the earth in two generations. 'They' have done an excellent job on us; Goebbels himself would not have failed to have been impressed.

Why have 'they' done this to us? What possible, fathomable reason could there be to have gutted England's capital city of its Englishmen? What on earth were our governors thinking? One thing is for sure though and make no error; it has been a deliberate act. I can already feel my blood heating and so I shall come back to this later, like a moth to a flame.

TWO

EUROPEAN DISUNION

No foreign prince, prelate, state, or potentate hath, or ought to have any jurisdiction, power, superiority, pre-eminence, or authority, ecclesiastical or spiritual, within this realm.

English bill of rights 1689

What lies, what totally wicked, spiteful lies we have been told in the cause of European Union. From Heath (the bastard) through to Cameron and his little friends, we have been nudged, misinformed and generally taken for a ride for over forty years. When Heath fulfilled his perverted task and signed us up, he assured a trusting nation that we would experience no loss of sovereignty although he had been privately briefed that the opposite was true. He lied. Plain and simple.

It is a peculiar trait of the English that as we *expect* our politicians to be untrustworthy we are able to forgive them their deceit. Even so, they are only supposed to mislead, misinform and prevaricate. Heath just lied; through his teeth, in Parliament and on the telly. He sold British sovereignty on a lie and got away with it. My God, his lies were common knowledge whilst he was still an MP, the Father of the House no less. He was paid and feted when he should have been strung up from the nearest lamp post, or fed bratwurst and snails until he exploded. Or strapped to a chair and poked with a stick until he repented, etc, etc. I'm sure you get the picture.

The bottom line is that Heath blatantly lied and should have been brought to book. He wasn't. Why? Why was his treachery allowed to go unpunished or even unacknowledged? It is not as if he was loved by the nation, I am yet to meet anyone who had the slightest affection for the fat toad. Enoch Powell won the election for him in 1970 and it was Powell who ejected him in 1974.

No, he was forgiven by the establishment as he had fulfilled the function required of him. No, again that is not quite right. He was *rewarded* by the establishment for fulfilling that function. The Brits wouldn't have 'gone in' on the truth so someone had to tell the lies. That was Heath. His job was to inveigle us into the proto EU knowing full well that the 'common market' was a mere precursor of the super state of his fantasy. Wouldn't it be marvellous? 'No more war!'

Well my friend, European wars did not start because nation states respected each other's cultures, economies and traditions. They started because one foreign power attempted to dominate another. Such conflicts haven't occurred in the past seventy years as we have all finally decided that they are a poor option not because we have signed pieces of paper. We've had pieces of paper before; they're just pieces of paper, not effective against tanks. We have also avoided conflict because, actually, technology has compelled us to do so.

Heath was a liar and a Quisling.

And a bastard.

Next up was Harold Wilson. A man leading a government with more Soviet agents than Uncle Joe could have mustered for his 40th birthday bash. A man who colluded with the kind of union bosses who would have considered the KGB a bunch of Tory wets. Our 'arold promised us our say but did so only on the understanding that he would rig things up for the correct result.

'Do you wish to stay in the Common Market?' he enquired fatherly.

Fair enough? Not quite. He was looking for an affirmative answer to a misleading question. Again, in the quest for the EU superstate all tactics were considered fair. Asking the public to have a say in their governance is a risky old business and not to be left to chance. A huge sum of taxpayers' money was spent on the 'Yes' campaign with state agencies taking a partisan position. What with the money and the misinformation, the 'No' team never stood a snowball in hell's chance. It was Manchester United versus Mansfield Town. It was Frank Sinatra versus Cheryl Cole. It was George Foreman versus Nick Clegg. The fact that the British didn't have a clue what they were letting themselves in for was an extra, added bonus.

So the British gave the 'right' answer and it wasn't long before the Kentish orchards started to come down and for the Grimsby fishermen to idle on the dockside. The straight bananas came next, or was it the cucumbers? I can't quite recall. Anyway, the media came into play blaming all the latest lunacies on a continent which was still strange and exotic to many Englishmen. But we know that our politicos were simply using (and often corrupting) EU diktats as cover for what they themselves wanted to achieve, the subsumation of the populace into a cowed, obedient and unthinking mess. Cox's Orange Pippin anyone? No, we don't want that fragrant, delicious rubbish. We demand Golden Delicious (actually they are green and taste like a census form).

Would Margaret Hilda Thatcher please step up to the plate? Now there was a woman who held a healthy distrust of the whole enterprise but the pro EU lobby had become so entrenched by the time she achieved power that the cards were pretty stacked against her. She tried but her victories were technical rather than glorious. She negotiated a rebate (of our own money) which meant we were being ripped off a little less than before. She irritated the hell out of Mitterrand and Kohl which was good fun and she pressed on the brakes as hard as the Foreign Office would allow. But, but, but. She acquiesced to the Bruges treaty which she knew was just another slab in the Yellow Brick Road and she failed to acknowledge (at least outwardly) that there was a case for a clean break which I suspect she must have considered. Any frustration she may have felt she took out on the Argentineans and Neil Kinnock.

People have now largely forgotten where she was when the guillotine fell upon her, on the Continent being difficult and attempting to sabotage the putative single currency. *This* is why she was knifed in the back; it had little or nothing to do with the Poll Tax or interest rates. She largely retained the support of Basildon Man and would probably have given Kinnock another beating at the next election. However, the pro-Europeans around her (the likes of Heseltine and Howe) were tired of her and wished for someone a little more pliable to push things forward.

We remember Jacques Delors don't we? You know, the French chap who was the chief advocate of the single currency. Oh how wonderful it would be!

Ein continent! Ein currency! Ein Fuhrer!

I still remember the likes of Clarke, Howe and Heseltine salivating at the thought and terrifying us with the supposedly dire consequences of failing to board the ship. The past year or two has rather pointed out their fallibility don't you think?

No, that's a little kind of me.

These people were spectacularly wrong about an issue for which they terminated a Prime Minister.

It has been nice to hear their various apologies for their treachery, nice to see them eating humble pie, eating crow, etc. I would have been out when they did so but surely men of such honour and decency must have attempted to atone for their idiocy.

No? Oh well.

Here comes little Johnny replete with eager grin, faux leather satchel and remnants of last night's Currie on his shorts.

Maastricht Treaty? I'll sign it! It's only a little sovereignty, a mere trifle of a millennium of independence. However, if you stop eating our hamburgers I will bring the Continent to its knees!

There was *talk* of a referendum on Maastricht although the establishment were never going to put such an unpopular concept to the people. Referenda, we were told, were not part of our parliamentary democratic process and so we couldn't have one. It may have escaped your attention but this assertion is verging on the Heathian in its insincerity. Do you know how many referendums have been held in this country over the past thirty years? One? Two? Three?

Actually there have been ten on various issues which is a little surprising considering that parliamentary democracy thingy Major spoke of. Can you recall one on which you gave even the smallest toss?

No?

Neither can I.

The latest was the alternative vote nonsense which was essentially a chance for us to change the way that we vote for the same villains as we did before. You didn't like electing Nick Clegg under the old, tired system? Now you can have a go at electing Nick Clegg in a shiny, new format. Aren't we lucky to be free?

13

The simple and obvious reason for not testing the nations pulse on the European issue is the knowledge that the desire to blow a large hole in the project is firmly entrenched in the British mind. Your betters would never condone asking for your permission to continue as they are not confident of scaring you sufficiently to extract the required answer. Indeed, if after forty years of propaganda you would still like to jump ship, then you are unlikely to change your mind now and they know it. Therefore, they will not ask, not ever.

Over in Ireland, things have worked out a little differently. Polls were called with confidence but hubris was rewarded with humiliation as the proles voted down the Lisbon Treaty (EU constitution). The result was accepted as the will of the people, for about an hour, and then plans were put in play to ask again only this time with a salacious grin masking the icy stare. Luckily for the Federalists, Irelands economy collapsed (strangely enough, largely due to its membership of the EU and the single currency) leaving the Emerald Isle adrift in a sea of debt and destitution. This was manna for the 'Yes' camp, to the point that even I wondered if perhaps they really were doing God's will. It was possible to now say to the Irish, 'sign or starve'. They signed, thereby giving up the independence that they struggled for centuries to attain.

Down with Cromwell! Up with Von Rumpay!

As the country's economy deteriorated, months of claim and declaration by the Irish Government came to nought as it had to concede to EU pressure to accept a bailout package. The Irish were faced with two stark choices. Either they took on another huge pile of debt at unwelcome interest rates or they refused and faced a funding crisis which could potentially force the country out of monetary union. They opted for the rescue deal and must now look to grow their economy quickly in order to avoid a spiralling debt trap. They are not going to able to do this.

If we disregard the complexities of the economic arguments, the situation can be broken down quite simply. If you have a large debt and cannot increase your revenue at a rate higher than the interest rate due on the debt, then, all things being equal, your debt will only grow bigger with each year that passes and the interest due will follow suit. The only way to break this vicious circle is to increase the monies available to you either by cutting spending or by raising tax levels. Or both, as indeed the Irish did in their emergency budget. The problem is that such austere measures tend to crush any recovery in growth leaving the nation under serviced, overtaxed and with ever increasing debt. My guess is that Ireland will one day have to default (at least to a degree) and then take the opportunity to re-establish their freedom of movement.

The sad fact is that if Ireland is in hock to the EU, if it is beholden to Britain, if it is being pressed or pressured on tax policy and public spending and if the country's politics are being dictated by Brussels, then Ireland can no more be a sovereign nation than can Lancashire. This is the planned endgame. It is certainly one of only two realistic options. As is becoming progressively clearer, the current stage of European economic and monetary union is but a stepping stone, a halfway house between the common market and the federal state. There cannot be permanent monetary union without central control of tax policy and without fiscal transfers. If the EU does not advance to its federal destiny then it must die. Ultimately, the key is Germany. If the Germans are willing to disseminate their wealth to Southern Europe, as New York does to Memphis and London does to Liverpool, then a single state is possible. If however, the Germans decide otherwise then one can reasonably assume that the Euro is doomed. There is simply no logic in the current arrangements.

As it has always been, the one great positive for the Euro is the huge political will to see it succeed. Many forces conspire against it, not least its impracticality but its sponsors will fight tooth and nail to save it. In due course we shall find out just how far they will go to do so.

It is true that Europe is our biggest export market but this is also part of our problem. We are attempting to grow exports in a trading area in dire straits when there is a world of growing economies to exploit. The Germans can see this and are far better positioned, having retained their industrial base in a manner that we poor Brits could only dream of. This disparity is probably a legacy from the second war. Germany was destroyed and had to modernise. We simply staggered on, grievously weakened but without the energy that is so often found in destitution. Our best firms are constantly under threat of takeover, often due to their relative lack of size. The Government has made some nod to this problem, looking to expand our trade with China amongst others. Our problem is that we simply do not have the products to sell. If it is possible to correct this problem it will take many years to do so. I think that this is why we really should be looking to lay off the City a little. True, it is great fun bashing the bankers and there is certainly room to gripe about the way the Square Mile comports itself. However, financial services are by far the biggest contributor to the economy and continuing to attack the industry can only further damage the country's financial position.

We need to continually remind ourselves of the cause of the recent financial disaster. Individuals borrow too much and their excess debt is passed onto the banks. The banks can't deal with it and so the bankers go to the Government. The Government doesn't have the wherewithal and so they look to the individuals who borrowed too much in the first place. This strategy can sometimes be enhanced by the Government extending the chain to some supra national body such as the EU which then goes back to the Government for the cash who then take it from the individuals. It's a great system with only one flaw: it's cobblers.

At the risk of repeating myself, the Euro as presently constructed is fatally flawed and must be reconstituted at best. Even our own United Kingdom could not retain its common currency without large and permanent redistribution of funds to the poorer regions and nations within it. A similar situation persists in the United States. It follows that Greece and Spain cannot remain in a monetary union with Germany without spectacular gifts from the Prussian pocket. As the Germans have strongly indicated that they don't think much of this idea, something will have to give at some point. As eviction of the weaker states would mean certain default on their Euro based obligations and a run on their banking systems, my money would be on the Germans seeking the exit first. There are no palatable solutions to the Euro problem but at least a German exit would offer the Euro laggards the dramatic devaluation they need. Germany could go back to being rich and beating us at football. There would certainly be a substantial 'hit' to any of the strongest nations should they decide to cut and run. Germany's own exposure to 'sub prime' sovereign debt is huge and terrifying. It would seem to be an impossible situation for them but such times are when the 'unthinkable' begins to be considered. Germany would suffer but survive and the removal of the need to cater to German interests would certainly benefit the poor relations.

You would have read of the bailout offered to and accepted by Greece. Effectively, a huge sum has been rounded up by the IMF, the Euro zone nations (mostly Germany) and other EU nations (mostly us) and used for the purposes of fishing the Greeks out of their murky pond. The newly minted monies were used to buy Greek debt to which was attached a 'Euro' guarantee. We were essentially seeing a load of old rubbish being transformed into high quality bonds by way of an alchemy that would leave Merlin's tongue dribbling into his cauldron. For my life, I cannot see how increasing Greece's debt even further is a responsible solution to the essential problem, namely that the country owes more money than it can expect to pay back.

If we see Greece as Europe's errant son then we have seen his rehabilitation take the form of locking him in the attic. He has a biscuit or two to sustain him for a while but it won't be long before he is banging on the door and screaming for his dinner. There is a strange evil dread of evicting failed Euro zone members, as if this was a bad thing! If a member nation lies, cheats and fabricates, why would you want to keep them in the club just for appearances sake? The Greeks have a temporary stay of execution but other weak Euro zone nations find themselves in similar difficulties.

The whole Euro project has been, and is, hugely ambitious. It was, and is, driven by political ambition and this is reflected by its excessive and dangerously optimistic membership. Remember that we are not far from seeing membership offered to a very dubious selection of Eastern European countries.

The ideal was that all the peoples of Europe would merge their interests and, over time, a balance and equality would emerge. Germans would spend more and relax a little. This would allow the Greeks and Spaniards the opportunity to beef up their industrial output and save like Teutons. The Italians would discover fiscal rectitude and the Dutch would fritter away their incomes on shiny shoes and ice cream. What *has* happened is that the Germans have behaved like Germans, the Greeks like Greeks and ingrained national characteristics and cultures have not dramatically altered just because everyone's banknotes have the same pictures on them. Surprise Surprise, who would have thought it?

We (like many nations) face a compound interest trap which can only be alleviated by high growth (unlikely), deeper spending cuts (probable) or default (inadvisable). As I write, Greece is further down the track than any other EU member but there are plenty of other countries treading the same path. The Greeks were the first to succumb and go to the IMF after the yield demanded from Greek debt breached 10% (on its way to 20% and beyond). The country has short term funding but assistance comes with a heavy price and we saw graphic television images of the Grecian's refusal to relinquish his unfunded, untenable standard of living. We can reasonably expect more of this.

It is a similar problem to that of Argentina's some years ago, which was also caused largely by that nation's use of a currency peg, in that case to the Dollar. The Argentines eventually left that 'union' and devalued their Peso, a course of action not immediately available to Athens. There is however, one future option open to a besieged Greek Government and that is to default on its loan obligations. Argentina eventually did just this and the yields on Greek debt would indicate the market's belief that Athens will follow suit. Greek debt would be even more onerous in Drachma but then if you are going to default, it hardly matters what currency you do it in. The Greek Prime Minister is refusing to even acknowledge the possibility of such a disaster but you just wait until the bricks start coming through his windows.

A similar fate stares other EU nations in the face and the Euro itself faces its first big test. It has always been my view that the Euro in its current form is doomed to failure and that opinion can only be strengthened by current events. Whether this view is correct or not remains to be seen but it would certainly take the most fervent of Cleggettes to be advocating British entry to the zone at this point. There are some who continue to do so. Do not approach these people alone.

Without a trace of embarrassment, the pro- Euro lobby did indeed leap upon our own little difficulties as further proof of our need to join the Euro zone, implying that our travails are the result of having control over our own destiny. The fact is that although we have made a muck of things this is no reason to sub-contract the job to our continental cousins. In any case, European interest rates had been consistently lower than our own during the boom and so we could reasonably have expected our indebtedness and overspending to have been worse if we had taken the Euro Schilling. This country's problems have more to do with our predilection for debt and living beyond our means than with which currency we happen to be abusing at the time. They may also have some correlation with the incompetent lunatic who held our purse strings for thirteen years.

It is also instructive to remember that not all Euros are equal. German banks will only accept payments in Euros issued by certain member nations and not by others. For example, an Italian bank wishing to trade with a German bank must settle in German Euros and not Italian. The Bond market also clearly appreciates the difference. A German bond will trade at a huge premium to similar bonds issued by weaker nations and there is a predictable pecking order; the French rate higher than the Belgians who rate higher than the Spanish and so on. The Greeks and Italians rate amongst the lowest which is saddening for classical scholars but sensible if you do not wish to end up with a garden shed full of Lira and Drachmas at some point in the future. Indeed, whilst British entry into the Euro Zone is possible if a way can be wriggled around the referendum commitment (they will find some ruse when required), we are just as likely to see the jumping ship of a member nation or two.

A truly honest politician would tell things as they really are. Our country has a very poor future without a revolution in the way that it is governed and a logical first step would have been to blow the Lisbon Treaty out of the water. If this had resulted in our leaving the EU, then all well and good, I suspect that such a withdrawal would merely be the catalyst for other nations to follow. It would also mark our ground and make the one point that needs to be made above all others.

Let it be clear that from this point on, our country will be run for the benefit of our people above all others. Let this principle guide every policy and spending decision and then we may all feel that we really are 'in it together'. As things stand, the Briton should be aware that he is likely to continue to be the fall guy for the political classes' failure and dubious agenda.

The EU budget discussions of 2006 opened with a British insistence that our rebate was not subject for negotiation, not at all, or in the slightest, over our dead body, etc. Negotiations then followed which culminated in an increase in our net contribution running into billions of pounds. However, we did manage to secure a commitment from the French to have a little think about the Common Agricultural Policy at some point if they can get around to it, maybe. If they have done so, they haven't mentioned it. One result of the deal was that Britain will be the largest net contributor of all twenty-seven member states in the enlarged Union. Additional £billions will need to be found over the course of the deal, a deal by which we shall have to borrow huge sums from one set of foreigners in order to pass them immediately to another set. It's all very clever stuff and only idiot peasants like us can't see the brilliance of it.

The French meanwhile successfully defended their farming budget simply by refusing to discuss it, a tactic that has always worked extremely well for them. There was also a wonderful story reported to the British public which was supposed to emphasise the benefits of the European Union and its trade agreements. Apparently, President Chirac could be forgiven his protectionist agricultural policy as he had become enamoured of wine produced in Wales. Mon Chirac had apparently ordered two cases of Celtic vino causing great joy amongst the valley vintners. Unfortunately and almost immediately, the story was denied by the great man himself and the tale was quickly exposed as pure invention. The story was always likely to be demolished within hours, so why on earth do they make this stuff up? Chirac also took the opportunity to lavish praise on his friend Mr Blair and on Britain for our contribution to the debate and for our flexibility.

All the proof you could ever need that we had been well and truly done.

When stranded under the ash cloud in 2010, I looked at my limited options of reaching England from the Canaries. Mr Brown instructed me to make my way to Madrid and then within two hours made it clear that under no circumstances should I make my way to Madrid. The Spanish authorities had declared that they would offer every possible assistance in my time of need. This seemed to entail charging E1500 per day to hire a four wheeled thimble which I would have to leave at the French border. The French railwaymen took the opportunity to go on strike. Viva La EU!

It was easier getting across Europe in 1944.

THREE

MY UNCLE WAS A HERO

Don't fight a battle if you don't gain anything by winning.

Field Marshall Erwin Rommel

On a recent visit to an elderly aunt I was leafing through the daily rag that she insists on buying and scanned the usual tales of violence, degradation and C list celebrity bull. Specifically, I read of more riots both here and across Europe. This 'news' was notable in that such events are only sometimes reported. A very great number take place across the continent only to be ignored by our liberal press. As you are 'internet savvy' I assume that you are aware of this. As Auntie made the tea, I glanced up at the wall and gazed upon the monotone image of my late uncle during his days as a Desert Rat. Not for the first time I was struck by his noble countenance and kindly features, family traits I would add. A real hero thinks I and it's true. You may have never heard of him but it is true. He never won a gong for conspicuous gallantry during his army service nor scaled the heights of commerce in peacetime but it is true nonetheless. No one ever wrote the book of his life and he had the common decency never to enter politics but I tell you that my uncle was a hero and I shall expect you to believe me. I'll not even tell you his name as it wouldn't mean much to you if anything. Even so, I would like to take a few moments to explain just *who* he was.

My uncle was born into dire poverty in 1920's London, East London to be precise. In 'Shit Street' he would have said. His first act of bravery was in enduring the poor hand that Lady Luck had dealt him without becoming bitter, hateful or indeed burning down the High Street. After our great but often neglectful nation had offered him such limited privilege, my uncle could perhaps have been excused the occasional bout of 'simply demonstrating his concern at the lack of opportunities for Cockney youth'. There are however, no records written or verbal, to suggest that local shopkeepers were ever subject to his 'understandable pent up fury' or his 'justifiable feelings of alienation'.

He added to his record of derring-do by not offering what would have turned out to have been a justified two fingered salute at General Churchill when called upon to serve his country. He exchanged cloth cap for dark green beret and became a Rifleman. Off he went to war, Blighty furnishing him with an ill-fitting uniform and a rather good chance of being rather dead rather quickly. He was sent into battle. He went. Along with his mates, he went.

I have often considered it ironic that, quite often, famed stories of courage concern the exploits of men whose daring deeds were not fuelled by bravery in its truest form. It occurs to me that oftentimes such men lack an essential component of true courage, that of fear. It is not possible for a man without fear to be brave. For me, true valour is not 'having no fear of death' but rather having the quite normal and overpowering fear of death and yet still be willing to risk your neck for a cause, a loved one or one's country. Therein lies the secret of our nation's glorious military tradition. It is not only our Nelsons and Drakes who have defended our shores so wonderfully for so long. We have also needed the legions of uncles' who swallowed their panic and faced front.

Anyway, back to the tale. My particular uncle spent much of his war in the desert. He fought in the big actions; Alamein and Colonel Turner's VC winning action at Kidney Ridge included and did his best to come home to those who loved him.

Happily, our hero survived the disagreement with Germany and he, much relieved, returned home. Or rather he tried to, the Luftwaffe having mistaken Shit Street for something of strategic importance. In concert with all the other uncles, he vowed to rebuild. Not just his little part of London but the whole glorious Jerusalem. He disdained the less tasteful courses of politics and high finance and pursued the far more honourable profession of 'working man', perhaps recognising that our great leaders are naught but windbags without the great working people (of whatever class). Our civilisation can only function on consent. My uncle gave his brave consent to work for the rebuilding of a dream. The terribly sad thing is that while he and millions of his kind were toiling to build the land fit for heroes, their 'betters' were conspiring to destroy their right to pass it on to their descendents.

Of course it's easy to be cynical today; after all we can look back at the past sixty years and see what a bloody mess we have made of things. The decline and decay can be seen in every town and city across the country. My uncle passed away many years ago, thankfully not fully aware of how far we have strayed from his hopes for us. To his last, he retained that beautiful sincerity that can still be found in those who remain of his generation. He was not for becoming embroiled into arguments of advanced economics or delicate foreign affairs. He lived a hero's life following a simple set of rules that have maintained civilisation in these islands for centuries. If they were good enough for his countrymen they were plenty good enough for him thank you very much.

I know that my uncle was only a hero in a relative sense. Relative that is to so many born after him. He himself was not particularly conspicuous amongst his brothers in arms but then they were a pretty heroic bunch. They were willing to stand up for themselves and their families and lived proud, decent lives. They recognised the need to work; indeed they pleaded and fought for work when it was scarce. They looked to improve their positions by the skill of their hands, to feed their children by the sweat of their brows. Never expecting that for all the material advances they made, their *quality* of life would be lower today than it was decades ago.

Older people have always looked back on their own time through rose-tinted glasses. Now however, it seems to have gone beyond pining for the good old days. There is a very real longing for the past on the part of younger folk too, a longing for the happiness and security that is found in real communities, for the feeling of safety in the home or the freedom to walk the streets after dark that existed in the past and does not do so now.

Although he is sadly missed, I'm glad that my uncle was spared the worst of today's excesses; I couldn't bear to have seen him peeping nervously through the nets. To have seen the scourge of Rommel concerned for his safety coming back from the Post Office. To have his hero's pride steadily eroded by the suggestion, perhaps even a realisation that his great efforts were not 'worth it'. It would have been too sad to see just as it is heartbreaking to see in those of his fellows that remain.

And so we have the choice. Do we wait for all of the nation's uncles to die, bury them quickly and move on? Or, do we take some inspiration from their heroism and re-learn that which civilised us? Do we re-discover the qualities of duty, sacrifice and consideration? Do we re-learn (for example) that unemployment should be railed against, protested, hated and fought but never used as an excuse to rob the old? Do we re-learn that a decent, civilised society is only possible if populated by decent, civilised people? Our schools should teach this kind of heroism. Uncle studies anyone?

It has occurred to me that documentaries tend to narrate the passage of my uncle's war quite dispassionately, almost neutrally. This is particularly prevalent on the BBC which likes to talk of 'British forces' as if they were from outer space. However, when any mention is made of 'Commonwealth' troops, then the music plays and the bunting comes out. Weren't we so very, very lucky to have such good friends to come and win our war for us? Shouldn't our eternal gratitude therefore extend to an open door immigration policy?

This old chestnut is long overdue for demolition. Of course there were non- white servicemen who fought, some with distinction and before we are regaled with tales of individual heroism from the Commonwealth, let us be clear that we are not discussing personal motivation. Personal motivation is largely irrelevant in the grand scheme of things. If we look at the thing dispassionately and from a remove of seven decades, it is clear that ultimately, practically, it was the British that fought for the world rather than the other way around. If what we are told about the Nazis is true, then if there was a single nation that stood a prayer of survival under the Germans it was the English. Not the Africans, and not the Asians, all of whom Adolf would have apparently enslaved and/or liquidated without a moment's hesitation.

This is why the constant carping at us is just so intolerable. If there are debts owed, they are owed to us and not by us. The sooner this is understood by an increasingly servile and idiotic nation the better our chances of a different kind of future. It is symptomatic of a deeper problem.

Decades of self loathing liberalism have brought us to the point where large numbers of our people feel themselves responsible for just about everything that has gone wrong in the world. We cannot hope for a future with a national mentality that is so susceptible to such stupidity. The English must, if they can, regain the sense of self worth that has seen us through our history. Would our people today even be capable of responding to a Churchill? I doubt it.

We have been subjected to a monstrous programme of liberal propaganda that has been tantamount to brainwashing. Our ability to withstand the tide of anti-British rhetoric will steadily decrease as we progressively lose any sense of ourselves within our islands. The English in particular have increasing difficulty in recognising themselves correctly. It is difficult, even dangerous today to be overtly English as liberalism prefers the more easily corrupted 'British' persona. Even so, a Somalian chap can be 'British' as he has been given the appropriate documentation. He could never be 'English' if he lived for a thousand years. Your masters know this, you do to.

FOUR
THE PEOPLE'S FRIEND

Nothing is so well calculated to produce a death-like torpor in the country as an extended system of taxation and a great national debt.

William Cobbett

Though passionate in his politics, William Cobbett chose to remain aloof from party. This independence allowed him to comment freely on any and every subject that appealed to him. He was branded an egotist by his opponents and there is certainly truth in that. It is also true that Cobbett held nobody's opinion higher than his own. He spent half of his life urging his countrymen to heed his advice and the other half berating them when they ignored him. However, Cobbett did have many graces that not only saved his character but which have also preserved his name to this day as one of the great reforming patriots. He was undoubtedly sincere in his cause, had an undeniable affection for his country and his people and, most important of all, he was (for the establishment) painfully right on many of the burning issues of his time.

Perhaps Cobbett's greatest talent was in taking the complex issues of the day out of the hands of those who preferred to keep exclusive control of them. He then relayed these issues in laymen's terms to the common people. Indeed, some of the great crusades in his ceaselessly crusading life were his attempts to expose and put a stop to the corrupt practices of the Government. He campaigned tirelessly to expose the abuse of Government funds to finance unearned pensions, going as far as to publish lists of names and figures in his 'Weekly Political Register'. Wouldn't it be lovely if someone would do this today? His hatred was strong for all 'tax-eaters' who fed off the high taxation that impoverished the common people. Cobbett idealised the poor but free Englishman and warned that there were fast becoming only two classes of man; masters and abject dependants.

Witnessing the poverty that seemed to be swallowing up whole counties, Cobbett clearly saw the need for reform in both the political and economic spheres. Consequently, (through the 'Political Register') he supported the Chartist cause, taking care however to maintain his independence. In an effort to reach the highest possible circulation he published a special edition of the Register, dropping the price from a shilling to tuppence to accommodate the poorest in the land. In this edition, 'An address to the journeymen and labourers of England, Scotland, Wales and Ireland', Cobbett broke down the argument and counter-argument of reform to its bare essentials, claiming that it was the burden of taxation that impoverished the people rather than any programme of industrialisation.

Cobbett urged his readership to support the reform movement but he also bewarned of the great dangers that awaited the cause. He urged Chartist leaders to renounce the violence that accompanied their activities and he assured them of success if they followed a more conciliatory path. This had the dual effect of both pleasing certain sections of the establishment and much paining others. The more cynical opponents of reform were perturbed by the concept of a peaceful, legitimate and well-argued case being presented to the King and Parliament.

They worried that the justness of the Chartists' grievances would find a sympathetic ear amongst the British Government and people. They feared Cobbett as one who could unite the common people both with each other and with other sections of society. Cobbett was certainly an early opponent of big government, Christening the term 'The Thing'.

This was an all encompassing name for borough mongers, pensioners, sinecurists, placemen and all other 'tax eaters'.

Though a committed reformer and a recognised radical, Cobbett took great pains to point out that he was no revolutionary. He wrote in 1809,

'I have had too much opportunity of studying men and things to be led astray by any wild theories of liberty... I want no innovation. All I wish is the constitution of England undefiled by corruption.'

An abiding quality of Cobbett's life and character was indeed his love of country. However, this patriotism took a different form from that of many of his political opponents. Cobbett saw loyalty to nation as indivisible from loyalty to family, people and the very land itself. He concerned himself far less with foreign adventures than with the preservation of the culture he so loved. In his works, he urged his countrymen to retain as much of their heritage as they possibly could. As a farmer, he gave his employees leave to observe all the old holidays and festivals, organising and sponsoring the manly Sunday sports which Cobbett believed bred strength and character.

'Love of country is founded in the value which men set upon its renown, its laws, its liberties and its prosperity, or more properly speaking, perhaps, upon the reputation, the security, the freedom from oppression and the happiness, which they derive from belonging to such country.'

This comment reveals much of Cobbett's thinking. He implored his countrymen to preserve their nation in trust for the next generations but warned the coming children that in return for the gift of country came the heavy responsibility for its care and preservation. Indeed, it was family affections that lay at the centre of his world. He believed in the hearth and the family table but beyond this he held that a bond of family existed between all those that made up 'his people'. It was this concept of family unity that landed Cobbett a two year prison sentence.

Though Cobbett had long been a thorn in the side of a government that itched to put him out of circulation, he had always managed to use his literary skill to avoid any charge of sedition. However, in 1810 Cobbett's patriotism was sufficiently outraged for him to misjudge his comments. Five militia men stationed in Ely had complained of a stoppage in their pay and had been flogged for their trouble. This was outrage enough but the fact that the beating was administered by German mercenary troops brought Cobbett to a state of near hysteria. To a man such as he, the idea of Englishmen being beaten in *England* by foreigners was totally unacceptable. He roundly, loudly and violently condemned the incident in sufficient terms to earn himself a charge of seditious libel and a subsequent gaoling. This danger of arrest and imprisonment loomed large over Cobbett for most of his career. His outspokenness in one of the most repressive periods of government in our history kept him almost constantly in a state of war, both with the Government of the day and also with those personal opponents that Cobbett fought a running battle with over decades.

Of these enemies, Cobbett reserved perhaps his greatest venom for William Wilberforce and their bitter exchanges provided much entertainment for the public. They clashed on virtually every subject though their mutual disaffection was based as much on personal dislike as on their political differences.

For Cobbett's part, he saw his piously religious opponent as the very worst kind of hypocrite. Wilberforce led the campaign to end the trade in slaves and to emancipate those slaves already in existence. Of course, no man should be in slavery and Wilberforce's passion for this ideal to become reality is well-known. Less well known however, is the extent to which Wilberforce was willing to *curtail* personal liberty, not for the Negro slaves but in regard to his own countrymen. For all Wilberforce's supposed love of freedom he supported or was responsible for much of the repressive legislation brought into being over the period during and after the Napoleonic wars. As the poor of England buckled under the weight of the Corn Laws and heavy taxation, the case for reform gathered strength under the leadership of Cobbett and others. Their demands for lower taxes, cheaper food and a reform of Parliament met with stiff opposition from the establishment of which Wilberforce was a leading member. As the clamour for reform grew louder, so the measures introduced to resist it grew ever more oppressive. At one point during the reign of George III there were over seventy capital offences. These ranged from highway robbery to impersonating a Greenwich pensioner. The former had wide reaching connotations; a woman in Manchester was executed for stealing potatoes from a cart.

In fairness, Wilberforce did oppose some proposed legislation to increase the number of capital offenses but in 1817, at a time of domestic unrest, he advocated the suspension of habeas corpus. Cobbett, and others who moved among the common people, understood that the desire for major insurrection was minimal. Those such as Wilberforce who had little or no contact with the people feared a bloody revolution and reacted accordingly. Wilberforce's support for the suspension of such an important safeguard of his countrymen's rights as habeas corpus was (for the reformers) hypocritical in the extreme. For did not Wilberforce preach so much on freedom? Sir Francis Burdett vented the feelings of his colleagues;

> *'I confess I am astonished at the concurrence in this measure of an honourable and religious gentleman who lays claim to a superior piety ... nothing could be more anti-Christian than to shut up persons in solitary confinement.'*

Cobbett however, was not quite so polite in his condemnation. Wilberforce was always a target for his pen and Cobbett's dislike for his adversary grew with every edition of the 'Register'. Cobbett constantly taunted the object of his distaste, lecturing him on every topic and punctuating his writing with comments such as;

'Now you will observe Wilberforce... Mark it Wilberforce, note it down.'

One of Cobbett's pet hates was Wilberforce's involvement in organisations such as the long winded 'Society for the Suppression of Vice and the Encouragement of Religion and Virtue throughout the United Kingdom'. This organisation sought, amongst other things, a tighter moral code and a stricter Sabbath. Cobbett saw an ulterior motive in this apparently pious organisation. He believed the movement sought to ban what Cobbett saw as the manly sports popular among the common people. To him, the Society was an attempt to extinguish the sparse pleasures and amusements of the poor. Cobbett accused Wilberforce of attempting to turn the poor into clean, sober and punctual wage slaves.

Again, contrary to Wilberforce's supposed love of freedom, he gave firm and vocal support for much repressive legislation. He strongly urged that the Seditious Meetings Bill should be passed and he lent his weight to the successful passage of the 'Six Acts', the last of which sought to tax the radical press out of existence. This act slapped stamp duty on almost all publications except those containing subject matter of 'piety, devotion, or charity'. Cobbett was quick to spot the loophole. With delicious insolence he published his work firstly as, 'Cobbett's Monthly Religious Tracts', then as 'Cobbett's Monthly Sermons'. To his eternal glory he actually got away with it! His 'Sermons' became regular reading for those who enjoyed Cobbett's attacks on his old foes, Wilberforce most definitely among them.

It is a great paradox that history sees Wilberforce as the traditionalist figure and Cobbett as the radical seeking great change. In reality, Cobbett wanted to maintain (or return to) the traditional ways and freedoms of England. For all his piety, Wilberforce used his position to support oppressive measures that were effectively stripping the Englishman of his long held and hard gained rights. The new Corn Law of 1815 drew a predictable division between the two men. Though Wilberforce claimed to have given the proposed law much thought, his decision to side with the agricultural lobby came as no surprise to Cobbett who mobilised support against the bill writing,

'There is something so monstrous in the idea of compelling people to purchase their food dear when they could purchase it cheap.'

Quite what Cobbett would have made of the Common Agricultural Policy we shall never know but can suspect.

The furore over the new law again increased the unrest among the people which Cobbett duly attempted to channel into a positive movement for reform. Wilberforce however, deeply mistrusted Cobbett's motives, commenting that;

'Of all the conspiratorial villains, Cobbett is the most pernicious of all.'

So the two men fought each other on virtually every issue but as we have seen, at the heart of their animosity for each other was a deep, abiding mutual loathing. Wilberforce hated what he saw as Cobbett's irreligiousness whilst Cobbett detested what he deemed Wilberforce's 'holier than thou' attitude. Indeed, Wilberforce's claim to have reached his decision on the 1815 Corn Law whilst at prayer sent Cobbett into paroxysms of anger.

35

If there was one single issue that divided them, it was Wilberforce's abolitionist campaign. Wilberforce has his place in history as a leading light in the struggle to end the trade in slaves. The commemoration in 2005 of Britain's abolition of the trade widely promoted him as a great hero of the oppressed and the impoverished. Though Cobbett also opposed the inhuman traffic in people, he refused to join the abolitionists who, virtually to a man, he labelled as hypocrites. Many of those that worked themselves into a frenzy on behalf of the African Negro happily ignored the grinding wage slavery that existed in their own towns and shires. Many of them grew rich from profits and dividends wrought from the pain and misery of their own people. Indeed, Wilberforce spent much of his opium raddled existence funded by the slavery of his own countrymen's children.

Though slavery was a great wrong, it is an unpalatable fact that by affixing a monetary value to a human being, that human being has some material worth. If a slave was brutalised or neglected in such a way as to cause his death or incapacitation it was necessary to replace him. This entailed a cash loss that the 'owner' would sensibly attempt to avoid. If on the other hand, a nineteenth century English child employed in industry became (through the neglect that society showered upon him) incapable of work, then his employer would simply replace him with a different child. So, although the African child was officially a slave and the English child officially free, a look at longevity and infant mortality records will more than blur the picture of exactly which of the two was better off. This was Cobbett's point. How could Wilberforce break his heart at the plight of the black American yet ignore the pain racked faces and crippled bodies of children worked fourteen hours a day at machines that could safely be described as lethal weapons?

Indeed, huge numbers of Britons lived and worked in intolerable conditions that would have been unheard of on the American plantation.

These conditions existed before the campaign for abolition reached its peak and they continued long after slavery was brought an end. To illustrate this point we can look at Jack London's 'The People of the Abyss' published in 1903, *forty years* after the end of the American Civil War. In this vivid description of English wage slavery, London writes of an elderly couple he came across in our capital city. These old people had lost their children either to the Empire or to disease and they found themselves unable to continue working. With no children to support them, they were driven to the workhouse where they were separated by sex. After a lifetime together, they bade each other farewell for in the workhouse there was no fraternisation between the sexes. Consequently, this old couple faced the probability of never seeing each other again.

It is true that many acts of great cruelty occurred in the slave states of America. In Britain however, such cruelty was a matter of procedure. So although Cobbett did not support slavery, he saw much to clean up in his own backyard before he looked across the ocean. *'Charity begins at home'* is certainly a maxim that Cobbett would have sympathised with. Quite what he would have made of some of our present day politicians is not difficult to gauge.

Though Cobbett never joined a party, he did finally enter Parliament in 1832 as he approached his seventieth year. Now in close proximity to his old adversaries, Cobbett demonstrated that though old age approached he had lost none of his fire and irreverence. A high spot of his three year tenure at Westminster was a short contribution to the debate on Lord Shaftesbury's reforming factory bill of 1833. Representatives of the textile industry argued that to reduce the working day of mill children from twelve to ten hours would ruin the industry and deal a mighty blow to the nation. Cobbett rose and claimed to have seen the light!

'We have this night discovered, that the shipping, the land, and the bank and its credit, are all nothing worth compared with the labour of three hundred thousand little girls in Lancashire! Aye, when compared with only an eighth part of the labour of those three hundred thousand little girls, from whose labour if we only deduct two hours a day, away goes the wealth, away goes the capital, away go the resources, the power, and the glory of England!'

Cobbett's efforts on this bill were of no avail but he spent the last two years of his life in similar campaigns. The Poor Law of 1834 brought predictable fury from the old campaigner. The bill proposed to introduce the workhouse as the only form of relief. For one such as Cobbett who always craved the sweet air, this was the cruellest of laws. Again his efforts came to nothing but he continued to campaign until his death in 1835. He had outlived Wilberforce by two years and Cobbett made no secret of his pleasure at surviving his old foe. The two men had fought a bitter war for many years and there was never any rapprochement between them. Cobbett hated Wilberforce and his loathing was returned. But Cobbett held the advantage in that he *enjoyed* hating Wilberforce and enjoyed fermenting hatred in a man who so dearly yearned to be a saint. One of Cobbett's most cherished achievements was in making Wilberforce hate him.

When William Cobbett died, it was at home as he wished. He was a man for whom land and people were indivisible. He believed that his people belonged to England and that England belonged to his people. Despite all the injustice that he fought, he believed that the laws, customs and people of this country were fundamentally good and that the preservation and advancement of this nation was paramount. We can be sure that Cobbett would have fiercely opposed our own twenty first century 'philanthropists'. It is becoming increasingly obvious that our modern day Wilberforces are having a calamitous effect on our society. It is a great pity that William Cobbett is not here to tell us why

So where is *our* Cobbett? A nation as inventive and creative as ours must have one, so where is he? By definition, he should not be afraid to raise his head above the parapet, so where is he? No such man exists that I can see although I confess that I do quite like Vernon Coleman. He certainly comes close to matching Cobbett's work rate and he is popular enough to be ignored and detested by the mainstream and this is obviously in his favour. You should read some of his books, I would particularly steer you towards his demolition of former Prime Minister Brown. The book is entitled 'Gordon is a moron' and is worth buying just to giggle at the title.

FIVE
SWIMMING AGAINST THE TIDE

Have you ever wondered, perhaps, why opinions which the majority of people quite naturally hold are, if anyone dares express them publicly, denounced as 'controversial', 'extremist', 'explosive', 'disgraceful', and overwhelmed with a violence and venom quite unknown to debate on mere political issues? It is because the whole power of the aggressor depends upon preventing people from seeing what is happening and from saying what they see. The most perfect, and the most dangerous, example of this process is the subject miscalled, and deliberately miscalled, 'race'. The people of this country are told that they must feel neither alarm nor objection to a West Indian, African and Asian population which will rise to several millions being introduced into this country. If they do, they are 'prejudiced', 'racialist'... a current situation, and a future prospect, which only a few years ago would have appeared to everyone not merely intolerable but frankly incredible, has to be represented as if welcomed by all rational and right-thinking people. The public are literally made to say that black is white. Newspapers like the Sunday Times denounce it as 'spouting the fantasies of racial purity' to say that a child born of English parents in Peking is not Chinese but English, or that a child born of Indian parents in Birmingham is not English but Indian. It is even heresy to assert the plain fact that the English are a white nation. Whether those who take part know it or not, this process of brainwashing by repetition of manifest absurdities is a sinister and deadly weapon. In the end, it renders the majority, who are marked down to be the victims of violence or revolution or tyranny, incapable of self-defence by depriving them of their wits and convincing them that what they thought was right is wrong. The process has already gone perilously far, when political parties at a general election dare not discuss a subject which results from and depends on political action and which for millions of electors transcends all others in importance; or when party leaders can be mesmerised into accepting from the enemy the slogans of 'racialist' and 'unChristian' and applying them to lifelong political colleagues...

J Enoch Powell

41

Perhaps the most pressing of issues facing England today is that of immigration. In order to examine the issue rationally, it is necessary to set one thing straight from the beginning.

It is an indisputable fact that the immigration experienced in this country since the Second World War has been imposed without the people's consent and against their wishes.

No consultation with the people was attempted and no vote was taken. It is to our country's eternal credit that its people have attempted to make a proper go of the enforced experiment but the fact remains that, had the people been consulted, mass immigration into Britain would not have occurred. A grasp of this truth is required before any discourse on this delicate matter is possible; otherwise our debate immediately lapses into misunderstanding, incomprehension and often hysteria. However, once the truth is acknowledged we can examine the causes of mass immigration and its consequences for our country.

A falling birth rate amongst Europeans is often cited as a major reason to encourage further and increased immigration into our communities in order to support our aging populations. However, it is both sensible and reasonable to believe that the decline in a nation's birth rate has some link to the economic and social forces that are imposed by mass immigration into that nation. Just as red squirrels will not breed when under pressure for space and resources, Europeans are extremely loath to produce the children needed to maintain an ageing population both because of the economic demands placed upon them and, directly or indirectly, by the influx of aliens into their towns and cities. A sensible and responsible young couple today (the kind we dearly need to have more children) are reticent to deliver these children into an atmosphere of poverty, unemployment and social strife.

Where (as in London) there is already a huge and youthful immigrant or immigrant descended presence, there are, as a consequence, intolerable demands on housing, employment and education. A (working) working class couple in particular have to consider many factors before embarking on parenthood. It is all very well producing children but the difficulty in finding a decent school to which to send them can be an almost insoluble problem. The same problems exist with regard to housing and employment and there is a very real fear of introducing children into an alien society.

One of the saddest sights is that of the urban Englishman trying to convey to his suburban countryman the difficulties of the multiracial city. No logic or emotion seems able to reach the one who does not have first hand contact with the melting pot. The suburbanite cannot understand why we can't just 'live and let live', and the townie cannot understand how the other can be so blind to it all. For two men of the same stock to be so incomprehensible to each other is terribly sad and is indicative of the divisions that have proved our undoing for too long. The enthusiasm that the provincial English have for multiracialism is directly connected to the degree by which they have to endure it. John Major may feel that mass immigration has 'enriched our culture' as he lives in Huntingdon but why did he move to that awful place? Brixton is lovely this time of year.

How it is possible to approve further immigration of working (or otherwise) migrants while every EU country is suffering chronic unemployment is completely beyond the comprehension of any rational and clear thinking man. Even if it were true that migrants were needed to bolster the work force, it would be one thing to allow aliens to work in Europe but quite another to furnish these workers with citizenship and settlement rights. The obvious consequence of naturalising large numbers of foreigners is that the alien population gradually (or otherwise) gains ascendency in economic, numeric and political terms.

In effect, a young European couple contemplating parenthood, after weighing up the consequences of having a child and the prospects for that child, may decide not to have that child at all. How many people do you know that have 'capped' their families for financial and social reasons? This couple in turn will age and require the state to support them. Having produced no offspring to fund this support, the pro-immigration lobby leap into action claiming more migrants are needed. Claiming in effect, that immigration is a solution to an ageing population as opposed to a major cause of it, our salvation as opposed to our downfall!

The first mass waves of immigration occurred during the nineteen fifties. We are told that this country was desperately in need of extra manpower in order to build up our country's shattered economy. The immigrants, we are told, were brought here to do the jobs that the British people didn't want to do. This is the story, the legend; the excuse for all that has come to us since. Perhaps there was some kernel of truth to it initially, I do not believe it but perhaps there was. However, it certainly hasn't been remotely true for at least forty years so we need to ask why mass immigration has continued and accelerated over that period.

Outside of the Second World War there has been no extended period in living memory where every Briton has had a job. Full employment is a condition that we have not enjoyed, other than when able to conscript millions of men into the armed forces in the expectation that large numbers of them would be culled. Under the present arrangements, it never will occur in this country. How can any mature economy expect to employ all of its potential workers and hundreds of thousands of new people arriving each year? It obviously follows that if, as in the 1990's, there were still millions of unemployed people there must be an ulterior motive to importing millions of migrants, working or otherwise. This suspicion was finally confirmed when it was revealed that the Blair administration opened the floodgates as a matter of policy. No condemnation can be attributed to the immigrants themselves. In the main, they were and are simply people attempting to improve their own lot. The responsibility for the present intolerable situation lies squarely at the feet of the politicians and businessmen of the 1950's, as indeed of every period since.

The simple fact of the matter is that with *relatively* few unemployed, the onus for social change shifted dramatically away from the bosses and their politician friends and finally towards the people themselves. This shift promised the British people a larger share in the fortune they had sacrificed so much for. It stands to reason that if it was difficult recruiting workers for the railways, it was not because there was no pool of unused labour to draw on but rather that the pay and conditions were poor. Of course, rather than give an Englishman a higher wage, the preference was to import cheap labour, so cutting wage bills and, of course, increasing the pool of unemployed giving business an advantage when the time came to negotiating the next wage round.

It is a widely held belief that post war immigration was a response to our labour shortage of that time. You may well believe this but there were other factors involved. We understand that the migrants came here to do the jobs that the British didn't want to do. If we take the most commonly used examples, the immigrants were needed to work in our health service and our transport system. Ok, sounds fair but we have to ask ourselves some additional questions.

- **Did Britons work as nurses and bus drivers *before* the war? And if so why did they want not to do so after 1945?**

- **Did they feel that these jobs were now beneath them? This is unlikely.**

It *is* likely however that they simply preferred to do other jobs that paid them more money.

So we've dispelled one little myth right there. The British workers did not refuse these jobs as demeaning; they refused these jobs as low paid. By extension, these jobs were low paid because there was an additional (and inexhaustible supply) of cheaper labour which would come in very handy with keeping down wage levels. The myth is perpetuated to this day with the stock, *'the British don't want to do these jobs'* line. The truth is nearer to, *'they don't want to do these jobs for the kind of pay that we can get an African refugee to do them for'.*

It was an anomaly of Britain's constitution that until the belated nationality act of 1963, there was no clear legal definition of who belonged to this country and who did not. Basically anyone who was a citizen of the Empire was eligible for a British passport and, as a consequence, had a right to enter the United Kingdom. Considering the size and population of our Empire at that time, this was obviously a huge gap in our border controls! The fact that it wasn't until 1963 that Parliament attempted to close this yawning chasm is an awful indictment of the tardiness of government in anything but raising taxes. And so, encouraged by big business eager for cheap labour, they came.

Of course, we have to accept that mass immigration has 'happened' whether we like it or not. I think that we could do a radically better job at dealing with its consequences but it has happened and we need to deal with it as fairly and rationally as we can. I can certainly understand the concept that our Islands are now no longer exclusively British, (and indeed that they are unlikely to remain predominantly British for awfully much longer) and that we have to deal with this new reality. I can understand this view. I think that it is often tainted with cowardice. We may be, *'committing the sin of fear and calling it the virtue of tolerance'*, as Chesterton put it, but I *can* understand it. However, the view that what we have now is better than what we had before is obscene, insulting and ridiculous. It can only be explained by treachery or mental illness.

It is also maintained that Britain is tired and needs the influx of new blood. What a gross insult this is. Does the nation of Nelson and Drake really need the third world to survive?

There *is* a link between birth-rate and the economic and environmental forces imposed by mass immigration. Allowing more mass immigration whilst keeping millions of British people on benefits is beyond comprehension without adherence to at least one conspiracy theory, maybe two!

The Labour Party could never redeem itself unless it returned to the basic principle on which it was founded; that is, to elevate the social position of the British working man. This is extremely unlikely to happen. Their thirteen year policy of intense immigration is a complete reversal of the original aim, as are the penal taxes imposed on the Englishman in order to finance the 'one-world' experiment. Admittedly, the Labour leadership were supposedly scholars and not scientists, for what scientist would strive to continue an experiment that had already gone tragically wrong?

While charting the decline of Labour's morality, we should remember that in the 1950s, the leading union leaders fiercely opposed mass immigration as cheap labour and a threat to workers rights and prosperity. Unfortunately, Harold Wilson's party quickly 'sold out' in order to land the immigrant vote. As we are all aware, since then the indigenous population of these islands has suffered wave upon mammoth wave of unwanted migration and the indignities that have accompanied them. The proponents of multi-racialism argue that their experiment could work if people would only forget their differences but forgetting differences does not make differences disappear.

Many of multiculturalism's advocates are ostensibly intelligent people. Of course, by definition, this is illusory. What scholar could find an example of a multicultural society succeeding in a way that triumphed over a homogenous culture? What scientist could conceive of continuing an experiment that has patently failed? Advocates of the Rainbow Nation ask us to suspend our grip on reality, to see something other than what is staring us in the face. What they are asking is not for Britons to forget differences but to forget their heritage and their birthright, their very selves. Our great sin is not failing to appreciate the merits of other nations but is in failing to recognise those of our own.

The general thrust of their argument is that we are really all the same, but how outrageous that they could suggest such a thing, what an insult it is to people of *all* races. Consider it for a moment. Do you truly believe that the only difference between yourself and an African is the colour of your skin? The differences in culture, in temperament and in sensibilities are overwhelming and obvious to any honest man. The Rainbow folk claim that Britain has been subject to immigration for a thousand years, long before black immigration but the European peoples that came and made Britain their home were Northern European peoples. They came in far fewer numbers and were far more easily integrated.

Consider the Apache, a defined group which is recognised, and freely referred to as, a separate and sovereign nation. Such nations are not defined by geographical boundaries but rather by the distinctions they recognise amongst themselves. The Zulu nation could be transported anywhere in the world and still be a nation, much as Israel is a Jewish nation though its people were drawn from around the globe. This is accepted and it is curious therefore that the same recognition is not afforded to the peoples of the Western world. Here, a nation is seen as a land mass defined by politically drawn boundaries. Why is this? Well, it is time to let loose the conspiracy theories as only these seem to make the slightest sense.

We have all heard of the proposed New World Order and laugh heartily at the concept largely because we cannot conceive of such an unnatural thing. Many of those who believe that the threat of NWO is real are undeniably lunatics who imagine the shadowy organisation to consist of secret cabals of Jews and financiers smoking Havanas and chortling at their dastardly plot like so many bad Bond villains. Unfortunately for us, there is some truth amidst all the fantasy. There *are* organisations dedicated to bringing about a world government and they are very real. The European Union is one. The Bilderberg Group is another and indeed, like the EU, its most important meetings *are* held in secret. George Osborne attends, Denis Healey did to and he of the eyebrows has openly stated that a single, universal government *is* a Bilderberg aim. The group's membership comprises some of the richest and most powerful people in the world and provides much fuel for the fires of the internet theorists.

It seems sensible to assume that for the new order to take shape, then nations and nationality need to be extinguished or at least heavily diluted. It is permissible for the Zulu and the Apache to retain their 'nationhood' because they are no real hindrance to progress. The nations of the West however are quite another thing entirely. There is not the slightest hope of 'one world' for as long as the established nation states of the Old World remain. Therefore, they must go, and by any means possible. The small third world nations can be mopped up later once the hard work is done.

It is necessary to strip the people of these nations of their patriotism and love of country in order to strip their nations from them. To achieve this, it is first necessary to confuse the citizen as to what his feelings for his nation actually are. He can be allowed certain outlets for his primitive patriotism on a transitionary basis but only particular and *inclusive* outlets and these must first be approved and authorised by his betters. He cannot be allowed to be confident of his ground. He can be permitted to wave a Bill and Kate tea towel at a royal wedding procession but he cannot be allowed to associate his love of England with the English themselves.

It is instinctively that we think of our nation and our people to be two sides of the same coin. This is not appreciated by the folks over at the New World Order club. We are bombarded with daily propaganda that our conception of nation and people is wrong. We are not wrong, we are just losing that's all.

> *The homogeneity of England, so profound and embracing that counties and the regions make it a hobby to discover their differences and assert their peculiarities; the continuity of England, which has brought this unity and this homogeneity about by the slow alchemy of centuries…From this continuous life of a united people in their island home springs, as from the soil of England, all that is peculiar in the gifts and the achievements of the English nation, its laws, its literature, its freedom, its self-discipline.*
>
> **J Enoch Powell**

The nation state is the highest form of government that can be endured before a descent into dictatorship. We are experiencing a deliberate blurring of the concept of nationhood designed to dilute the natural patriotism and survival instinct that may allow us to oppose our destruction.

To see Cameron play the immigration card before the 2011 local elections was as sickening as it was predictable. The man has not one intention of dealing or seriously engaging with the issue although we are at least alert enough at this stage to see his blatant electioneering for what it is. What was interesting however was to see many of the interviews with members of the public that appeared on TV at the time. Virtually to a man and woman, the interviewees agreed that immigration was out of control, that it was frightening them and that they would like to have it addressed. What was even more of interest was that only some of these people had white faces. We shouldn't be surprised at this, why would someone support the disintegration of our borders simply because he happened to be black or brown or whatever? People from all sections of society understand that immigration concerns are, and always were, a question of numbers. The sad thing is that Cameron would have seen those interviews and still will not act.

Why? What is so wrong with such people that they cannot engage properly on this issue? Is it some kind of middle class colonial guilt issue? Is it fear? Is it an actual desire to see us usurped in our own land? I ask these questions in a genuine spirit of confusion, the mentality of these deluded souls is so alien to me that I have racked my brains my whole adult life in an attempt to understand what goes through their heads. My suspicion is that there must be some unhealthy, self loathing guilt trip going on. This is only a suspicion as these people will never come clean and tell us straight what their motivation really is.

The intellectual distinctions between patriotism and nationalism are essentially a con trick. They exist to confuse the thoughts and emotions of the people. I suspect that most of our countrymen could not explain the difference between the two concepts and those that can are only parroting what they have been told by those who are neither nationalist nor patriot. Can you ably define the difference? I don't think that I can and this is the best that I can come up with.

- **Support your national hockey team and you are a patriot.**
- **Ask for your borders to be policed and you are a 'nationalist'.**

Cameron looks to peddle the confusing 'distinction' as hard as any of his predecessors. Should he try to palm this off onto you, you should be ready with one of two stock answers, both of which are equally rooted in our English character and both of which are equally fit for the purpose. If you are genteel, well read and well mannered, you should explain softly that you are not concerned with such piffling semantics and you consider them to bordering on the dishonest. Everyone else should tell him to piss off.

England is not the state, it is not the institutions and it is not the Monarchy. All these things are 'English' only because they derive from the people who regard themselves such. They are of, and belonging to the people. Perhaps one cannot live without another but they are not one and the same. England can only live with her people within her, the English people.

True patriotism can only be for a nation of one's own people, the phony distinctions between patriotism and nationalism are part of the attempt to separate the English from England. They should be resisted with every ounce of our remaining strength.

SIX

THE GREAT LIE MACHINE

In left-wing circles it is always felt that there is something slightly disgraceful in being an Englishman, and that it is a duty to snigger at every English institution, from horse racing to suet puddings. It is a strange fact, but it is unquestionably true, that almost any English intellectual would feel more ashamed of standing to attention during 'God Save the King' than stealing from a poor box.

George Orwell

I once counted the numbers of non whites on the BBC's children's channel. Over the course of two hours viewing with my infant daughter, I noted fifteen different presenters and do you know how many of these were 'white British'?

One, and he was an idiot.

Does it matter about the colour of a presenter's skin? If it does not, why does the BBC go to such extreme lengths to gerrymander the number of visible ethnic minority employees? Fourteen out of fifteen is a huge percentage considering that non-whites are still a minority across the country as a whole. Why then?

If the world's great dictators were sat in a schoolroom, then it would be little Adolf who raised his hand first to answer this one.

'Get zem young, get zem young and zey vill be mine forever!'

As with the Hitler Jugend so it is with Auntie. If the infants and children of Britain can be blitzkrieged with multi-cultural images, drenched in other cultures and brainwashed to believe in the one world utopia, then they shall grow to be model citizens of the shambolic, crime stained, hateful hell that we are stumbling towards.

My eldest daughter came home one day and corrected me for some mildly off colour remark. Her teacher had apparently primed her and her peers to watch out for and to reprimand any sign of parental prejudice. Hitler did that, he really did, exactly the same thing. He instructed his 'youth' to observe their parents and report any sign of 'anti-Nazi' sympathies.

Stalin did it too, and so did the other great figures of the left. We're doing it now, more subtly as befits a more sophisticated age but we are doing it. At least, the left is doing it. Do you think that they are likely to stop doing it unless we make them stop? Do you not think that their subtleness might grow into full blown tyranny unless we do not prevent it from doing so?

I am not optimistic about this. You simply cannot trust the left to have any sense of perspective or proportion. This sort of thing never ends until some other reactionary body makes it end. The Weimar Republic was amongst the most decadent of Western regimes. The Nazi Party was, in some ways, a nervous reaction to it. Left wing 'liberalism' always ends with the Gestapo. What I am advocating is for decent, civilised people to end it before we reach the *'I will close my eyes and ask no questions as long as you make it go away'* stage.

> All I have ever heard from the mainstream is that there is a 'conversation' to be had regarding immigration but which never, ever actually occurs. What the hell do they expect people to do?

There are some media commentators who occasionally air the concerns of the English at the accelerating decline of their civilisation. I often wonder about the true agenda of these people as they do seem to have all the hallmarks of establishment safety valves. They rail against the lunacy of our immigration policy but constantly plot against any real clear opposition to it. I find it more than odd that they condemn mass immigration for the disaster it is but still look to steer their readership away from any effective protest. What solutions are they proposing? Is it this fanciful notion of a mass movement of 'nice' middle class folk that will rise up to end the madness in an orderly fashion?

This is especially irritating as it has now been confirmed that Labour's policy of swamping us in immigration has indeed been a deliberate act, thus confirming what those 'beyond the pale' have been saying all along. However, the media's strategy seems to continue as follows;

- **Admit that immigration is out of control.**
- **Lambast the main parties for perpetuating it.**
- **Destroy anyone opposing it.**

Supposedly conservative journalists have been getting away with this for decades. They encourage their readers that someone is speaking up for them but are always careful to steer their readership away from any effective dissent. They really do need to be careful that they don't lose all remaining creditability in the same way as the words 'racist' and 'fascist' have lost much of their power through overuse. But then the naivety and gullibility of the English *is* quite astounding, supposedly intelligent people whose only conception of an 'English patriot' is that of a foul-mouthed, shaven-headed drunkard. Surely people should not simply accept this grotesque media caricature without question? They do, it's easier than independent thought.

It is a matter of taste of course, but I'm not too keen on parts of our imported culture either. We have vast swathes of British youth dressed like morons, talking like morons and listening to awful 'music', like morons. It is always interesting to watch the leftists/ feminists/ Marxists 'getting down' to rap songs that implore them to 'beat their bitch', or to murder people in order to achieve an increase in income, or even perhaps to acquire the victims own 'bitch' in order to slap her around a little as well.

The promotion of this stuff is a deliberate policy on the part of the leftist music industry and the liberal media. People, especially young people, can be trained to like whatever we want them to like. If we create an impression that it is 'cool' to like rubbish and 'un-cool' not to, then the young will like rubbish. This applies whether they like it or not, if you know what I mean.

Even supposedly sensible people affect to enjoy 'songs' which lambast them for their white racism or for their whiteness itself. It's a little like a black fellow buying the latest 'Knights of the Ku Klux Klan' long player. What the hell is wrong with these people? Some of the best popular music in history has been created by black artists. I listen to it and I enjoy it but then Chuck Berry never told me that he was coming round to shoot me and enslave my wife.

SEVEN

ABOVE THE PARAPET

In the beginning of a change, the patriot is a scarce man, and brave, and hated and scorned. When his cause succeeds, the timid join him, for then it costs nothing to be a patriot.

Mark Twain

It may be interesting to look at one or two examples of politicians who admitted to seeing what was being done to our nation and who found the courage to speak out. It is certainly instructive to note their fate.

Let's start with the obvious; Enoch Powell caused perhaps the greatest hoohah in British politics when he transposed the deep concern of the British regarding immigration into words and deeds. An old style patrician Tory, Powell managed the extraordinary feat of extracting support and affection from both the shires and from the inner city. He had perhaps the most powerful intellect of any post war British politician which at least exempts him from the shaven headed, drunken Nazi label. He also began the Second War as a private soldier and finished it as a Brigadier which, to my mind, gave him the right to say anything he pleased. Of course what he is really remembered for is the series of speeches he gave in the late 1960's culminating in the 'Rivers of blood' speech that effectively ruined him.

It is largely forgotten that a policy of voluntary repatriation was (supposedly) seriously mooted within the opposition Conservative Party of 1968 and Powell was only elucidating the genuine fears and suspicions of the people. However, our old friend Heath (the bastard) was somehow his boss at the time and did what was necessary to ruin Powell within the party. The Tories went along with this in their usual lazy fashion although it would be interesting if we could ask Powell's colleagues of the era if they still felt that they made the right choice.

It has always puzzled me how the Parliamentary Conservative Party would have chosen an intellectual pygmy like Heath over Powell, or indeed over any other sentient being when selecting their leader but I suppose that it is a pointless exercise to try to fathom it out. The important thing for us to remember is that Powell's comments on immigration drew huge support from every strand of society with a very substantial majority of the population indicating their approval. This, as always, horrified the established political class and it was therefore necessary for them to remove him as far away from power as was humanly possible. Again, we need to remind ourselves of the anti-democratic nature of this established cabal. The people wanted Powell and thus he had to go.

Powell himself was surprised by the degree of support he received from the 'working classes'. He was the definition of highbrow and certainly not a natural man of the people. However, this rather odd man touched on a nerve that jangles to this day.

The people of Britain do not want mass immigration and never did. The situation in 1968 was not anywhere near as pressing as it is in 2011 but public opinion was clear then as it is clear now. Powell stated that the immigrant population might even reach two million at some point. He was roundly condemned for such alarmist predictions by opponents who knew full well that this was a pathetic understatement of what was coming our way.

My appreciation for Powell's courage is tinged with my disappointment with his later career. He parted with the Tories over their pro Common Market policy and then effectively isolated himself in Northern Ireland.

58

He could have done so much more. He could have stood in his Midlands constituency as an independent. He could have stood in an Inner London constituency causing all sorts of valuable mischief. Ultimately, he gave a snivelling political class what they wanted, he walked away and this is a great pity, for him and his legacy, and more so for us.

Sir Oswald Mosley was wrong about many things but he was right about many others. Not many people will tell you that. Mosley is seen as so far 'beyond the pale' that it is taking your life into your hands to even consider that the man was anything other than a Nazi-obsessed devil who would have had Krauts in Westminster and death camps in Scotland if he had got his way. I bring him up mostly because I am not supposed to but also to re-emphasise an earlier point.

Mosley was wrong to go fascist in 1932; it was a spectacular error of his political judgement. This is true even if the fascist 'brand', though dubious at the time, did not have the overwhelming connotations that it has had in the post war era. He was wrong to wear a uniform and he was wrong to respond to attacks from wealthy Jewish financiers by condemning the Jewish people as a whole.

However, he was right about unemployment in 1929 when everyone else was wrong. He was right about resisting the push for war against Germany in 1939 and he was right about immigration in the 1950's. Failure to deal with unemployment meant misery for millions in the 1930's, entry into a cataclysmic war meant misery *and* death for millions in the 1940's and failure to address immigration has meant misery for millions ever since.

Of course, as soon as we were dragged into the war with Germany, Mosley was finished as a political force. His black shirt would never be forgiven or forgotten and he spent the last forty years of his life in rueful bewilderment as his worst fears were played out.

Mosley is remembered now as some sort of pantomime villain in grainy monotone images that are wheeled out whenever the populace stirs and murmurs concern over the state of the nation and needs to be slapped down. *This* is why he is mentioned here. He is used as a bogeyman to educate the public of the dangers of right wing sentiments. It is conveniently forgotten that Mosley formed his new party after leaving Labour when he felt that it could not cope with his radical socialist ideas. So essentially, we have a man who sought to usurp parliament re-dressed in right wing clothing for public consumption. When you hear of him being condemned as a right wing monster you might wish to recall that Mosley was a man of the left. He said so often enough. The next time he is used in an attempt to stifle your legitimate concerns, you should remember this.

Joseph Chamberlain is one of those great historic figures who were fundamentally important in their own eras but who have been largely forgotten today. Chamberlain was a colossus in the late Victorian age offering positive solutions to the questions of the day which, had they been adopted, would certainly have made a radical difference to our history.

From his stronghold in Birmingham, 'Radical Joe' held forth on issues ranging from the provision of basic utilities to the reform of the tariff system that perverted trade within the Empire. Indeed, tariff reform was a major issue of the time but one which was fudged repeatedly and never satisfactorily resolved. Chamberlain's idea was for 'imperial preference', to reduce and eliminate tariffs for the Empire nations in order to create an efficient, mutually satisfactory trading zone to the benefit of Great Britain and its dominions and colonies.

The workshop of the world would take in the raw materials and produce the quality manufactures required around the globe. Considering the vastness of our Empire and our clear access to every conceivable resource, it was a sound scheme. Unfortunately, as ever, it butted up against the vested interests of home and abroad and was never implemented. It was a golden opportunity missed and the question of Empire trade was never settled in any logical fashion.

At home, Chamberlain voiced dissent against many of Britain's foreign adventures although not necessarily from an anti-imperialist standpoint. Rather, he often opposed the regular conflicts as he believed that they diverted Parliament and the country's attention from the myriad of problems at home. This was a sentiment that Cobbett would have shared and which seems to have achieved some real traction today. As Britain and her people require some real attention, perhaps it would be a reasonable idea to stop haring around the world shooting at folk.

Although passed over for the (Liberal Party) leadership, Chamberlain was still very much 'in the game' and still a potential Prime Minister when he was struck down by a major stroke in 1906. He struggled on until 1914 but his political career was effectively over. His eldest son enjoyed a lengthy stint in Parliament and younger son Neville had the misfortune to be Premier in the late 1930's. However, it was Joseph that the country needed but who was denied to us by the usual political manoeuvrings and the cruel hand of fate.

The treatment of these people and their effective banishment has served a great and useful purpose for those who would plot our downfall. One cursory look at what happened to these men is very instructive to any politician who might toy with the idea of raising an objection to our progressive extinction.

'You shall be destroyed as they were destroyed'.

Any man or woman, having invested years of effort in reaching the House of Commons or even a council chamber is unlikely to risk a similar fate. Therefore, and almost inevitably, we have a self perpetuating stream of culpable politicians willing to place their own interests over those of their nation.

EIGHT
OH WHAT A LOVELY WAR

The right and proper thing, of course, is that every good patriot should stop at home and curse his own country. So long as that is being done everywhere, we may be sure that things are fairly happy, and being kept up to a reasonably high standard. So long as we are discontented separately we may be well content as a whole.

GK Chesterton

It was becoming a matter of years rather than months since we had volunteered for another war and it was therefore a blessed release when the Arab revolts began. It may well be over by the time you read this but as I write we are still embroiled in the Libyan situation with no apparent plan. We are not (we are told) interested in regime change in Libya which is none of our concern apparently. However, we are not going to stop until there is a change in regime within that country. One minister, when asked to predict the likely duration of the conflict helpfully responded, 'how long is a piece of string?' I suppose that this is as sensible an answer as one could reasonably expect but it remains a tad on the vague side.

If only we could summon the same enthusiasm for industry as we do for a punch up then perhaps we wouldn't be in quite the pickle that we find ourselves in. Apparently, we are almost out of Tomahawk missiles because we can only afford a few. It's a little akin to a bailiff turning up at your house with holes in his shoes and an empty soup can in his hand. With Gaddafi sitting on $Billions in gold and with porous borders to his south, he could quite possibly hang on for some time strengthening the 'case' for troops on the ground. I hope there *is* a plan this time. Even if the fun is over by the time you read this book, I can guarantee that we will soon be feeling around for another 'cause' to embroil ourselves in.

A grudging respect has to be offered to the Colonel for at least he is not the bland, autocratic despot of the type ejected in Egypt and elsewhere. He is a real, genuine, authentic and mad as a March Hare dictator of the old school. His speeches are genuine lunacy; he will happily drag people from their beds and he has that, can't be faked, mad gleam in his eyes. He may be evil, but ersatz he ain't.

For me, it has been interesting to learn that Libya is actually populated with people other than Germans and Englishmen. My only real knowledge of the place had been gleaned from my dear and sadly missed uncle who spent his youth blowing the place up. It had never really occurred to me that there were people there other than Northern Europeans moving armoured vehicles around. You don't see them in the movies and my uncle never mentioned them. He was never very keen on the place (too hot, injurious to his physical well-being and ridiculously few pubs) and I don't suppose much has changed.

Delving back to that time and as I alluded to earlier, there seems to be a slowly growing feeling in Britain that perhaps the Second World War was not such a great idea after all. We all know that the Great War was futile and counter-productive but many now consider that perhaps the more popular second conflict was a bit rash too. Alan Clark often referred to this possibility (for which he was roundly condemned) and there were many of Churchill's contemporaries who thought that perhaps we should have paused, had a cup of tea and weighed up the potential consequences of our intentions. Certainly, Neville Chamberlain wasn't keen although his reputation has suffered ever since. Here I would point you towards Pat Buchanan's work, 'Churchill, Hitler, and the Unnecessary War' which makes a strong case for our having gone off a little half cocked. Of course, Hitler was a real problem in 1939 but not necessarily *our* problem, certainly at that time. I often wonder why folk were so outraged at the German push into eastern lands in the late thirties; it is not as if Adolf had concealed his intentions. In fact, he had

had the decency to write his plans down for us in his rather dull book. Did we not have a translator to hand between 1923 and 1939?

Central and Eastern Europe has always lacked geographic and political permanence. Indeed, the twentieth century has seen a catalogue of new nation states being formed, some ridiculous when considering the ethnic makeup of the people affected. It is often difficult for the British to understand the continuous shift of territory and allegiances between the European nations. As an island race, we have always known the definite limits of our territory, our borders clearly and unalterably defined by the seas that surround us. We may still hanker after Calais but deep down we know that it doesn't belong to us, well *not really*. We are also consummate cartographers and for a long time reserved the right to adjust the world's borders if it suited us or if we became a little bored. We still like to try our hand at this today if we get the chance. Consequently, we are infuriated when foreigners don't stay between our lines. Can't they read the signs?

It is important that we understand that there is a different mentality in continental Europe, especially in the East with large slices of territory having been in dispute between two or more peoples for hundreds of years. In 1939, war was declared (at least nominally) in defence of that part of Poland which was stripped from Germany in 1919. It is often forgotten that while Germany invaded the portion of the relatively new state of Poland to which they felt they had a valid claim, the remainder of that country was annexed by the Soviet Union. The twin perils of Nazism and Bolshevism were effectively closing in on each other. Why on earth did we want to get in the middle?

Indeed, Hitler's other claims; the Sudetenland, Austria and the Rhineland were all arguably at one time German territory with ethnic Germans forming if not the majority, then certainly a substantive portion of the populations. This is not to say that these territories rightly 'belonged' to Germany but simply that they were the subject of legitimate dispute between peoples other than our own.

I am no apologist for Germany. My sole concern is the interests of my own country and I simply do not believe that defeating the Germans was reward enough for the sacrifices we had to make to do so.

Apart from anything else, the 'guarantee' to Poland was a stupendous exercise in hubris. How the hell did we expect to expel the Germans from a battlefield that we could only reach by travelling a thousand miles via Berlin and Dresden? We entered into a war which we had no hope of winning alone, and entered it alone. Was this courageous and moral or just plain stupid? Shall we liberate Nepal today with the fourteen soldiers we have who are not already otherwise engaged in some far off land?

It is likely that Hitler would have turned on his erstwhile Soviet allies rather sooner if he did not have the matter of Western Europe to deal with first. It is also likely that the German and Soviet armies would have exhausted themselves over several years of vicious conflict. As both regimes were extremely unpalatable to us, from a realpolitik point of view it might have been rather handy if they had. They might even still be at it today. The corporal wouldn't have knocked over the Russians as easily as he did the French and we could have spent the duration preparing ourselves for the possibility that the war might come our way at some point. We would certainly have been rather better prepared with a year or three to think about it. We might have had some planes and things to go with the blood, sweat and tears.

It is quite interesting to examine the drive for war from a safe distance. There was opposition to it in Parliament and not just from the pacific, there were also many public figures concerned with the obvious dangers of such an undertaking and a vocal if disunited peace movement. Even Mosley's BUF organised rallies urging peace and it did so until the summer of 1940 when it was banned and its leaders gaoled. It is instructive to read released Home Office papers that examined the English Fuhrer's campaign and deemed it 'little threat to the war effort'. What does this mean? I consider that the authorities felt that a 'movement for peace' was only acceptable if it had no prospect of success. By extension, should it have begun to succeed in persuading the British that this war was a really, really bad idea, then it would have been stomped on with Storm Trooper like savagery. The war was on, the war was wanted and the war would be fought. Initially, this would be with a First War Lee Enfield and a cardboard tank but, hell, something will turn up.

It did of course, turn up I mean, in the form of an international effort to smash Germany which performed the service of ridding the world of an evil empire and replacing it with; an evil empire. We saw the liberation of Eastern Europe from a vicious dictator and its deliverance to; a vicious dictator. We should remember that Stalin was responsible for a death toll that would have made Adolf blanch and that the Soviets held the world in fear for the next forty years. It is an unpalatable truth that if we could see a list of our war aims of 1939 then we wouldn't need much ink to tick off the ones that we succeeded in achieving; even Churchill was a little disappointed apparently. We did, however, manage to get our cities flattened, our vaults emptied and our empire mortally damaged. I can live with that. However, we also managed to get hundreds of thousands of our young men, women and children killed and countless more disabled, bereaved and mentally scarred. This I cannot live with at all.

Whilst not denying that Germany had designs on other lands to which they had no legitimate claim, we need to accept that the ever shifting balance of power is an inevitable consequence of Europe's confused racial make-up. If, in our disgust at Serbia's apparent dominance in her region, we assist the Croatians and the Bosnian Muslims to defeat Serbia, we will not have righted a wrong but merely replaced it with one of our own. We prevented the strong from defeating the weak by helping the weak to defeat the strong. Perhaps, as the weak became dominant with our help, we should have swapped sides to assist the Serbs!

It is now apparent that war crimes were not confined to the Serbian side alone but were common to all factions in the conflict, just as the Libyan rebels seem to be carrying out atrocities to equal those of Gaddafi's troops. Illegal acts are committed by many nations without recourse to action by the United Nation's Security Council. It is puzzling that the UN has never dared to interfere in the affairs of the Soviet Union, China and other powerful nations. It seems strange that Europe and the United States in particular were so eager to intervene in Bosnia, yet will not challenge China's right to occupy Nepal or insist that Turkey vacate northern Cyprus. We may *'move behind the scenes'* of course, we worked hard to sabotage the USSR's invasion of Afghanistan yet still thought it would be a cracking idea to have a go ourselves.

Incidentally, Noam Chomsky once pointed out that there was a great deal of fabricated atrocity propaganda in World War One. I know a little about this. In the late twenties the League of Nations issued a statement denouncing these claims as mere wartime propaganda as they were damaging international relations and the propagators, the US, UK and others freely admitted that they were a load of old cods. These claims included the 'eating of babies' and the 'raping of nuns' which I'm sure that you are aware of. Some which you may not be so familiar with were the 'drinking of blood' by German guards and the 'gassing of prisoners in hermetically sealed gas wagons'. It's funny how the Germans were exonerated of these wicked acts after the first lot and then decided that actually they were a really good idea in the second. Makes you wonder doesn't it? Well it does me.

Only now that that the wartime generation is almost gone is it possible for me to make these observations. I consider myself a patriot and would never, ever wish to disparage the efforts and sacrifice made by a generation of Britons so obviously superior to my own. No amount of revisionism could ever detract from their achievements. Unfortunately, I have always pondered the logic of it all and have fretted that we could perhaps have chosen a less destructive way of dealing with the genuine problem of Herr Hitler and his hordes. We knew nothing of death camps in 1939; we had no idea of the lengths that Germany would go to in order to secure its ends. On the basis of what we knew in 1939, going to war was a grievous error and only our pride in our eventual (pyrrhic) victory prevents us from acknowledging this sad fact. What is the point of all this?

The point is that this bloody disaster has been used as ammunition to justify the post war campaign against us and to further the aims of the left.

Don't want immigration?
Nazi! Nazi!

Would you please just keep an eye on the border then?
Fascist! Fascist!

Well, could I at least see a Christmas tree in our town centre?
Hate crime! Hate crime!

It's not that I wish we had lost the war, not at all. It's just that I think that actually we may have done so and are only beginning to realise it.

The Battle of Britain was twenty-three years ago and the world has forgotten it. Those young men, so many of whom I knew, flew up into the air and died for us and all we believed…What did they die for? I suppose for themselves and what they believed was England. It was England then – just for a few brave months…the peace which we are enduring is not worth their deaths.

England has become a third rate power, economically and morally. We are vulgarized by American values. America, which didn't even know war on its own ground, is now dictating our policies and patronizing our values.

We are now beset by the 'clever ones', all the cheap, frightened people who can see nothing but defeat and who have no pride, no knowledge of the past, no reverence for our lovely heritage…perhaps, just perhaps – someone will rise up and say, 'That isn't good enough.' There is still the basic English character to hold on to, But is there? I am old now. I despise the young who see no quality in our great past and who spit, with phony left-wing disdain, on all that we, as a race, have contributed to the living world…I say a grateful goodbye to those foolish, gallant young men who made it possible for me to be alive today to write these sentimental words.

Noel Coward

The Soldier

If I should die, think only this of me:
That there's some corner of a foreign field
That is for ever England. There shall be
In that rich earth a richer dust concealed;
A dust whom England bore, shaped, made aware,
Gave, once, her flowers to love, her ways to roam,
A body of England's, breathing English air,
Washed by the rivers, blest by suns of home.

And think, this heart, all evil shed away,
A pulse in the eternal mind, no less
Gives somewhere back the thoughts by England given;
Her sights and sounds; dreams happy as her day;
And laughter, learnt of friends; and gentleness,
In hearts at peace, under an English heaven.

Rupert Brooke

NINE

PARTY PARTY

Three groups spend other people's money: children, thieves, politicians. All three need supervision

Dick Armey-U S Congressman

If I were to trawl through the dubious histories of the mainstream political parties I would not finish this little book in a hundred years. I will therefore attempt to stay broadly in the modern era where, in any case, there is more than enough ammunition to shoot dead the entire political class. Their incompetence and treachery are bad enough but almost equally galling is the sheer rank stupidity of many of them.

We have endured over a decade of a lunatic Labour government which whilst hideous and destructive, did at least throw up the occasional moment of Chaplinesque high comedy as befitting such a troupe of outdated clowns. My personal favourite occurred in a Kentish constituency in 2005. The sitting Labour MP was informed by his own supporters that it was clear he would be unseated. Disgusted, he offered a nearby TV crew an interview in which he conceded his defeat and laid blame for said defeat squarely at the door of Tony Blair and his Iraqi adventure. Unburdened of the need to demonstrate loyalty, this soon to be jobless politician revealed his pent up hostility to Blair and cast doubt upon his integrity. Two hours later and following a recount, this gentleman was declared the victor with much building of bridges ahead of him. He immediately committed himself once more to the great Labour cause. You couldn't make it up.

Blair is somewhat of a tragedy. This man had the charisma to carry a nation with him and had such large majorities that he could have achieved great things should he have had the courage to do so, or if he really gave a fig. The pursuit of power is a scary thing; those that engage in it will always need watching closely and Blair more than proves the point.

He presided over a government that flooded the country with cheap foreign labour that would be directly pitched against his own 'working class' supporters.

He allowed the madman next door to raid our pensions, to sell off our gold reserves for a song and to generally cripple what had been a thriving economy. He involved us in so many wars that I can't recall them all and he subjected his country to human rights legislation which hobbled the justice system in its occasional attempts to protect the public from burglars, murderers and terrorists.

In the end, his final betrayal was in allowing Gordon Brown his turn at Number Ten. Blair knew that Brown wasn't fit and that he would cause incalculable damage to the nation. He knew and we know that he knew that Brown was unstable and more suited to Bedlam than to Downing Street. He knew and he did nothing to stop it. Tony Blair now tours the world in a private jet; he should be swinging from a lamp post.

Long before his resignation, he toured the country like Frank Sinatra on a farewell tour. It was classic Tony Blair to say such an emotive goodbye without actually going anywhere. We suspected that he wouldn't last a full third term and one had to be rather suspicious of his wish to do so. You can bet 'the bloke next door' was. It very much remained to be seen if Gordon Brown could achieve the improved public persona he desired, especially in Southern England. A metamorphosis into the kind of easy going sort of bloke you would lend a tenner to would have proved quite some renovation, perhaps a rival to Volkswagen's transformation of Hitler's 'People's Car' into Herbie the Beetle.

Brown purported to have become a nuke loving, commie hating conservative Englishman, or so the spin doctors would have had you believe. His campaign to succeed Blair (unopposed preferably) was spearheaded with his overtures to Middle England although it was fair to wonder whether he might not have left things a little late to have any kind of long-term and successful premiership, as if that were *ever* possible. At best, he would inherit an increasingly factionalised Labour government with a substantial but not conclusive majority. His own idiotic economic policies were storing up trouble for us all and would inevitably come to haunt him in No 10. Blair certainly saw it coming. We also had the West Lothian question reappearing, stronger perhaps than ever before. The visage of a Scottish Premier imposing high taxes on the English and distributing them amongst Scots who were beyond his power but not his largesse, was an outrageously unfair and insulting situation which should have had English MPs up in arms. Rather predictably it didn't although I believe that one or two did grind their teeth a little.

Brown's last budget as Chancellor purported to offer tax cuts to demonstrate the success of his policies. Chancellors of all hues tend to bribe the public before a General Election. For Brown to have attempted to do so mid-term was unusual but predictable. It was typical of him, representing as it did a blatant ploy by a public servant to use public funds to increase his own chances of garnering a better job. Brown would probably have gotten away with his slight of (under) hand a year or two previously but it appeared that he had been rather rumbled by this point. His fiddling around with personal taxation relied on the sleepiness of the taxpayer for success and, at this stage; people were beginning to watch his hands much as they would a bad conjurer. The various mirrors and smoke employed were par for the course and are of little interest. The costs to business of altering systems, salary runs, etc, most certainly are not.

Even so, perhaps such indulgent trickery could be forgiven if we had actually received a cut in our taxes as Brown intimated was the case but sadly no. It was effrontery on a grand scale to announce tax cuts that actually increased the tax burden and a disgraceful, though predictable end to a long standing chancellorship. Mr Brown may well have become the next Prime Minister but I always fancied that he would not enjoy his tenure. The public mood seemed to have turned upon him and only a few poor deluded souls were still willing to accept his frauds at face value.

Several years later, after laying waste to our finances, this incredible creature had the brass balls to lobby for the top job at the International Monetary Fund. Isaac Asimov would have deemed this fanciful.

John Prescott however, entertained us on practically every occasion he opened his dribbling mouth. On one occasion, he was found to have failed to pay his council tax whilst 'in charge' of the persecution of people who didn't pay their council tax. Of course it was just an oversight on his part; he was incredibly busy as Deputy Prime Minister, what with the affairs and the cars and the croquet and what not. We can therefore be generous and accept that he is not the total cretin that rational people consider him to be and that he did not deliberately attempt to evade tax. That said, it is verging on the astonishing that someone in Prescott's position would allow himself to be exposed to such a situation by his own department which was responsible for imposing the tax in the first place. For the Deputy Prime Minister to have backed the imprisonment of various elderly priests and octogenarian refuseniks whilst failing to cough up himself was classic Prescott. The story also gave the Press another chance to detail his regal lifestyle and residential glories. Hugely embarrassing for him but great fun for the rest of us and richly deserved for a man who was perhaps the densest entity ever to achieve high office.

I did in fact reach the point where I was simply incapable of putting pen to paper without comment on the music hall act that was Two Jags. The situation with this man moved from the ridiculous to the surreal via the downright embarrassing. Infidelity, corruption, and that (probably the most publicised in history) croquet tournament, all covered by a rabid press and yet he still managed to survive, with no real job, and advancing hippopotomonstrosesquipedaliophobia. It may well be that certain elements chased Prescott for his lack of social graces. In this case, I think that this is perfectly acceptable and does not constitute snobbery. My own background is as humble as the next man's but I would still prefer to be represented by someone who doesn't lick his fingers at diplomatic dinners.

A strange thing happened in 2008 when the Conservative Party achieved a most miraculous feat. Somehow they permitted Labour to re-invent itself as the City's friend whilst Cameron's opposition wailed in the wilderness, eschewing low taxes and advocating higher spending. Meanwhile, opsimath of the Century Gordon Brown toured the Square Mile pledging cuts in red tape and continuing 'support' for big business. I appreciate that politics is a chess game but quite how Cameron could have allowed someone with Brown's atrocious record to paint him into such a corner is quite beyond me.

The promise of a new wave of policies came to naught as the Brown administration hit the Northern Rocks in the autumn of that year. Policy statements were a mishmash of stolen clothes (Inheritance Tax reform), class envy (non domiciles taxation) and knee jerk fiscal policy (Capital Gains Tax reform). In fact, the Brown honeymoon period was over quicker than an Englishman's Wimbledon and he began to discover that a man cannot control things which he has allowed to get out of control.

We discovered that there was nothing so certain to enrage Brown than *not* being in control. His power lust made Stalin look like a Lambeth outreach worker. His petulant reaction to criticism and clumsy handling of various crises did not auger well for a statesmanlike premiership. It certainly seemed that by this stage the administration had run out of any ideas (even their trademark stupid ones) short of borrowing money. This should not have come as a complete surprise as Brown had already achieved the zenith of his ambition. He had become the Prime Minister. His only other remaining goal was to remain the Prime Minister. I don't consider that very much else entered his mind.

It was interesting to note and now recall the scandal over the funding of the main political parties which spread from the Labour Party to the Tories as sure as night follows day. If I have it right, the shared party line went like this;

We can't attract sufficient donations from people not looking to further corrupt us, so we have had to take cash on the sly instead. We are actually doing the people a favour by breaking the law as the alternative is the funding of major parties by the taxpayer.

Well actually, no it isn't. The alternative is going without; with a smaller HQ perhaps, maybe fewer spin-doctors and other creatures of the deep. If a political party can't legally support its framework then it should start to dismantle it. What actually happened is that the major parties were and are experiencing the financial effects of the public's apathy towards politicians and the political process. This apathy had shown itself at the ballot box in poor turnouts and could only be expected to translate into fewer donations and quite right too. Quite why the oily likes of Peter Hain felt that their rejection somehow proffered the right to the public purse was and is beyond me.

The kind of taxpayer funding that Hain suggested would be good for us would have contributed to the eternal perpetuation of the current 'old gang' political system. It would have secured the position of the mainstream parties and ensured their solvency regardless of how bloody useless they revealed themselves to be. If a party is bankrupt, let it go to the wall. If its debts are crippling, let it be crippled. If a party is unpopular and financially illiterate to the degree that it finds itself in near bankruptcy, where is the logic in bailing out such incompetents in order that they may run one of the biggest economies in the world? If market forces were good enough for the Farepak savers then they are plenty good enough for what are essentially privately run and owned pressure groups. They have no more right to public funding than the Women's Institute or Crewe Alexandra Football Club.

Anyone travelling abroad from 2008 would have been struck by the depreciation in the great British Pound. There were many reasons behind the fall but paramount was the realisation that our economy was somewhat of a basket case. One wag was heard to say that the UK escaped banana republic status only by dint of its monarchy and climate. I wish I had come up with that. We had, and have, a huge national debt, a chronic current account deficit, high taxes and low productivity. What funds we raise disappear into a bottomless pit of outmoded public services and we only get by with unsustainable borrowings and the constant introduction of new and ever more disingenuous taxes.

Currently they come under the guise of green levies but they are what they are; further extractions of cash from those deemed docile enough to bear them. Brown led us into an awful mess; the Pound was even being referred to in the City as the British Peso.

It was imperative that he be removed as it was obvious by this point that Brown's tenure as Prime Minister was unlikely to be one that anyone could enjoy without a generous supply of class A narcotics. The money boom was over and the Treasury now faced a new set of economic circumstances with empty coffers and very little in the way of fire power. Brown had also got himself into a mess over all sorts of issues which one suspects his predecessor would have side stepped neatly. Among the bloomers was the abolition of the 10p income tax band which so enraged many 'Old Labour' MPs. We also saw an attempt to force Catholic MPs to vote in favour of embryonic research. It doesn't matter what your personal views on the matter are, it was very poor political management and once again showed Brown's heavy hand where a Premier requires a deft touch.

The Brown Government also alienated large sections of the nation by its dishonest handling of the European constitution referendum issue. The Government insisted that the Lisbon treaty was fundamentally different from the original constitution document (it was not) and that our signature did not entail a further erosion of national sovereignty (it did). We were told once more that in our parliamentary democracy, Parliament is better qualified to take such decisions than are the voters. We were told once again that referenda do not constitute part of the British way. It is strange then that referenda have been offered to Scotland and Wales in recent years and indeed the promise of a referendum was offered in Labour's 2005 election manifesto. Sadly, the political lie is something that we have learned to live with, like rain soaked Julys, delays on the Underground and Harriet Harman.

Labour simply did not want the will of the people to interfere with its plans and with the promises it had made in private to its European colleagues. Such conduct devalues our democracy and continued such abuses will put its very existence into question.

There was an attempt to remove Brown but he used every Machiavellian manoeuvre at his disposal in order to stay in situ. If Brown has one great talent, it is that he is the consummate plotter and is extremely effective in dealing with those who would plot against him. Smear, stitch up and slander were all energetically employed to kill off the putative putsch. That said, it was surely a close run thing. For a few days, with the Downing Street lights dimmed, I was minded to compare our dear leader with another, earlier exponent of blind faith over rational assessment. Both men retreat into their bunkers, moving non-existent armies (or cabinet colleagues) around on an ever deteriorating battle map. Both live in denial and dream of the secret weapon that will surely turn the tide of history. One pins his hopes on space rockets and death rays, whilst the other waits for the triumph of his economic policies. The death ray was the likelier of the two.

Brown continued to stagger on with pointy finger and death grin. Why did he keep telling children that his father was a minister? Why did he persist in forcing out tears with the power of an Icelandic hilltop? It always seemed likely that he would require a larger lachrymatory soon enough but he was still in there thrashing around, playing the game against great odds. He stuck to his task almost religiously (well his father was a minister apparently), getting his sound bites across through the oft used tactic of constant repetition. Constantly repeating yourself does have a way of corrupting other people's minds, like the best advertising slogans, or ABBA.

Whether Brown's devotion was fuelled by conviction or insanity is a matter for historians and his therapist. However, I do remember sitting open mouthed in front of the television watching footage of the British Prime Minister orating, whilst accompanied by Elvis Presley (in the background) singing *The Wonder of You*.

'When no one else can understand me, when everything I do is wrong.'

Did I really see that? Was he mad? Was I?

One of us was, you decide.

There is no real need to go into the expenses/second home/ e-mail scandals, which rocked Parliament. It is perhaps a factor of my naive and rather romantic ideal of senior politicians that I believe they should be working twenty-hour days, alienating spouses and children alike in their Herculean efforts to keep the leaky SS Britain afloat. I did not for a moment begrudge Jacqui Smith the 88p but did rather wonder how she had the time to shop for bath plugs when the country was going to the dogs, hell in a handcart, down the Swannee etc. The expenses debacle inevitably resulted in political casualties although these were certainly not confined to the Labour benches. The media coverage of the whole sorry affair was such that it is quite easy to become blasé about exactly what had gone on. We should always remember that a swathe of cabinet ministers (including the Home Secretary) had to resign in disgrace. We should never forget just how enormous the whole affair became and the fury it inspired. Certainly it is just as well that Harriet Harman did not succeed in convening her 'court of public opinion' as Parliament Hill would have more likely resembled the lonely hill of Golgotha.

The wonderful Tommy Cooper once told a joke about separating a pub full of people into two groups; fools on the left and idiots on the right. We can use a similar tool in attempting to solve of one of life's great riddles; why do people vote Labour? I don't understand it. Are they mad or just thick? I know some mad people who are very intelligent and a number of thick ones who are very sensible. Perhaps you need to be mad *and* stupid to support the Labour Party, but then there are so many that do that they cannot all be stupid lunatics surely? Working on the assumption that they cannot *all* be such, then there must be some other explanation.

Perhaps it is due to some family tradition thing, you know, *'my father voted Labour, and his father before him, so I do.'* Well, this kind of sentiment would put you firmly in the camp of fools so we need to look elsewhere.

Maybe it is, *'I believe that the Labour Party represents the best interests and aspirations of the British working man.'* This kind of thing would place you squarely with the idiots so that's not it.

What about your feeling that Labour's historic record in government encourages the belief that they are a rational choice for another go? If you believe this then you need to be placed in the centre of the two groups and beaten senseless with a history book.

What's left? Oh yes, the spite and envy you feel for anyone who has a higher standard of living than you do even if this other person has worked his tail off to achieve it. This is quite a common one but whilst it is deeply unintelligent, it is more pathetic than mad.

That's it. I can't think of any more possible, plausible explanations as to why the citizens of this country continue to support Labour against overwhelming evidence that the party is congenitally useless to us. It is left for us to collate the evidence, to sift it, to weigh it and to attempt to summarise a phenomenon which has always puzzled and perplexed me. Ultimately, there can be only two real reasons why people persist in this compulsive behaviour.

They either have a vested interest in it, or they are as thick as mud.

Notwithstanding its own inherent idiocies, Labour has become the vehicle, the Trojan Horse in fact, for countless pressure and political splinter groups from the Militant Tendency of the 1980's to the myriad, disturbing one issue crackpots who have embedded themselves in every town hall and council chamber in the land. The party of Attlee and Hardie is a long distant memory and what we have today is a dangerous, treacherous combine of various factions which is dedicated to the destruction of the traditional way of life in this country.

Amongst others, we have the feminists who look to deny the undeniable, biological fact that men and women are different from each other. Both have strengths and weaknesses and the weaknesses of one are compensated by the strength of the other. It is this complementarity that allows a family to operate successfully. Dissolving the complementary nature of the partnership with the fanciful notion that males and females are somehow 'equal' in every way has radically altered our society and not, that I can see, for the better.

The great movement to 'liberate' women has had sadly predictable results; millions of broken homes, millions of single parents and millions of abortions. Ardent feminists write their books and live with their cats in Hampstead. Their victims live with their children, on benefits in

Barnsley. For here is the great paradox of the sexual revolution. The shift to remove the stigma from sexual activity hasn't liberated women at all. It is men that have been liberated, liberated from responsibility towards their partners and offspring. The women have still been left, literally holding the baby.

The removal of social stigma from many aspects of social activity has been hailed as an unmitigated good and indeed in certain instances it is welcome. However, stigma is also the glue that binds people to certain codes of behaviour which in turn shape an ordered society. Its virtual abolition is responsible for a widespread collapse in behavioural standards.

Incidentally, why are 'feminists' often so masculine? Surely a feminist should comport herself in pastel shades and a rather fetching pair of heels?

'Men's' issues are also integral to Labour's theology although the issues that it is concerned with tend to involve militant men with no interest in women, feminine or not.

'Ethnic' issues are big too (surely we are all ethnic are we not?) Apparently the big idea here is that the way to achieve integration and harmony is for everyone to separate themselves into their own groups along racial lines and then fight one another for resources.

Each 'group' has its own concerns and agendas but they all seem to share one mortal enemy; the white, heterosexual male, the evil, racist, misogynist, blood sucking white man who enslaves and exploits all others. You may be rich, you may be poor, you may be powerful, you may be weak and infirm but if your skin is pale and you quite fancy girls than you are the devil incarnate and that's a fact.

The way we are often portrayed on the television, as either weak minded or weak bodied (or both) would tend to contradict the 'evil racist, misogynist' thingy but conqueror or conquered, there is this feeling that somehow there is something wrong with us. Oh yes, we work and pay our taxes, we keep the wheels moving and maintain society but somehow there is something not quite right. England was, as we know, a cultural desert before 1948.

I don't feel particularly evil, my eyes are reasonably spaced apart and I wear no black moustache. Am I a misogynist? I have a wife and I have daughters. I have a dear mother, a sister, and numerous female relatives that I am extremely fond of. I adored both of my grandmothers. I live with females and I get out of bed in the morning to provide for them. I employ women and I am employed by them. That said, I am not big on the hoovering and so I remain open to challenge.

Am I a racist? I suppose that I am in the modern, perverted sense of the term. I feel no animosity towards those of other ethnicities but am very tired of having to qualify every statement with such platitudes. I do find that my instinctive affinity for my own kind (well, some of them at least) tends to rub up against the apparent need for me to give up on my own culture for the preferred mish-mash of differing and inassimilable cultures that the powers that be insanely imagine could gel into a cohesive whole. However, my skin is disgustingly white and I have a penis so I am indeed Beelzebub and have no place in the golden tomorrow.

I often daydream as to what might happen should all the straight white men leave the country (an awful lot have gone already). What would happen to all the 'groups' without their common enemy? You can wager that the feminists would be thrilled and delighted. The militant gay men might miss us for a while but would swiftly move on, by definition to

86

their own extinction. The 'ethnics' would probably throw a celebratory party before turning around and setting upon each other like cats in a bag.

How the hell have we managed to swallow the belief that a shift to the right from the left is inviting extremism? Let's take a little look at some of those awful 'conservatives' who have scarred our history. There's Lenin and his protégé Joe Stalin. There's Pol Pot and Papa Doc (not forgetting Baby of course). Mao se Tung was a noted fiscal and social conservative. Do we see a pattern emerging?

Adolf Hitler was a National *Socialist* as, at a stretch, was Mussolini. Even our very own Sir Oswald Mosley was a man of the left. The BNP is a party of the left.

There is something in the very essence of a socialist that drives him to control and dictate, to strive to forge men into his own contorted vision of what a man should be. He will brook no doubting and no dissent. He will go to any lengths and commit any crime in order to achieve his goal for he is sure of his messianic mission. He is sure that any methods are acceptable for he knows that ultimately the world will be one universal brotherhood dedicated to the common good. It is the purest bullshit of course, an ideology that so ignores the human condition can only result in the disaster that socialism always, always brings.

The future isn't bright for the English male. It really, really doesn't look good. It is scant consolation that the future for everyone else without us is even gloomier.

David Cameron is essentially the foppish flip side to Tony Blair. It is known that Cameron admires Blair and indeed models his approach upon him. His attempts to show himself as just 'one of the people' have bordered on the laughable. Does anyone really expect the British Prime Minister to go on a three star package holiday? Does he not realise that such stupidities do not impress but rather embarrass us? A year of Prime Minister Cameron has not demonstrated any evidence that he is any less the metropolitan liberal than Blair was.

Does he not wish to deal with the epidemic of burglaries that plagues our homes and families? Prison may not be a completely effective deterrent but it is a vastly superior one to a spot of community service and a bit of a talking to. What is so wrong with ensuring that people who believe that they have the right to rape our homes and terrify the elderly are sent down?

Of course, if we did that then we would need more prisons, so, er, let's build them. A burglar is unlikely to be able to burglarise whilst laid up in the Scrubs. Giuliani proved the point in New York and transformed that city from a stinking, crime infested hell hole into one of the safer cities in the United States and he did it in a surprisingly short time.

Prison doesn't rehabilitate? So what? Nor does letting people get away with criminal behaviour. At least your home won't be invaded by the same man again whilst he is banged up.

There was recently a case of a failed asylum seeker who had conducted a series of appeals against his deportation that stretched back over a decade and which involved hideous expense to the taxpayer. Why doesn't Cameron deal with this nonsense? If his hands are tied then he needs to stop bleating about it and set about freeing himself.

The fact is that Cameron is not a true conservative, not even a little bit of one to tell the truth. His birth decreed that any political ambition that he had would be channelled through the Conservative Party but he is essentially a liberal who is only roused to genuine passion when opposing the right. He has no intention of enacting conservative policies and principles, nor does he wish to do so. He regrets the supposed cuts in public spending but introduces them because he acknowledges that they are necessary for us to avoid instant insolvency. However, a true conservative could and would make the excellent case for cutting the dominance of the state as a matter of principle.

Talking of principle, he still cannot be forgiven for reneging on his promise of a referendum on the Lisbon Treaty (EU Constitution Bill). The treaty is now part of EU law of course but so what? The agreement was signed off by his predecessor in a most dishonest fashion, Brown also breaking a referendum pledge. Are we to be held to such dishonesty by convention? It is mere convention after all. If the British Prime Minister wishes to question the validity of a treaty then he can do so. *If* he wants to of course, which Cameron patently does not.

And what is the great Cameroonian idea? The Big Society! Somehow, we are all meant to pay more, receive less and still find it in our hearts to celebrate the unity of a chronically disunited nation. We are too far down the line for this nonsense to even achieve creditability as an idea. Any prospect of achieving a 'Big Society' in Britain died the day the Windrush docked at Tilbury.

The general election result of 2010 actually suited Cameron rather well. A slight Tory majority would have exposed him to the small conservative section of the Parliamentary Conservative party and he did not fancy that one bit. An alliance with the Liberal Democrats allowed him to drop many of the conservative ideas that ill suited him and afforded him cover to pursue his Blairite programme of managed decline. Watching him stroll hand in hand with Nick Clegg through the doors of Number 10 should have perturbed every man and woman that voted for him. He looked far, far too happy with the outcome, for my taste at least. He will go down in history as the man who snatched defeat from the jaws of victory and smiled. Dropping a twenty point lead against a ludicrously unpopular opponent, without murdering an old lady, is a fearsome achievement.

We are seeing a fracturing of the popular vote, with smaller parties (notably UKIP) affecting outcomes far more than they have in the past. We may well see this phenomenon persist as a feature of our political system, which could land us with a more 'Mediterranean' style of governance. Still, perhaps government is overrated. The Italians have one of the world's largest economies and have not had a stable Government since Mussolini danced his last dance.

And so to Sobber Clegg himself, a man of education but not of intelligence, a man of ideals who has no idea. He is a man without the strength of mind, body and character to withstand the pressures of office but one who is now the gel that holds the British government together. He is someone that the people behind the scenes will need to continually prop up and fortify in order to keep the wheels turning. He is a boy so completely out of his depth that he weeps when people are mean to him. He is a deputy Prime Minister who doesn't realise that he is in charge when Cameron is on holiday. Oh for the return of John Prescott, at least he could have a scrap.

The green lobby has its ideological roots in Marxism. It has picked up all sorts of converts along the way but it is Marxist in concept and origin. An awful lot of its activists have histories in extreme left organisations. Their dream was to control the world and its people through the wonders of communism. Oh dear, the wall has come tumbling down and the Soviet incubator has had its plug taken out. Oh well, experiment over then. Well not quite, perhaps it would be possible to find some other 'ism' that could be used to prevent the capitalist dogs and their lackeys from driving nice motor cars?

Eureka! Let's tell everyone that they will burn to a crisp unless we return to the dark ages. Let's make people sort out all the packaging and waste they didn't want in the first place into little piles and punish them if they don't do it properly. We can make up the rules as we go along to ensure that this happens.

We can chuck all the little piles of crap into the same hole eventually, that doesn't matter. The point is to make people do it, to train the little peasants into submission so that they won't complain when we start applying the 'green' taxes that we can use to continue the process of enslaving everyone.

We can build windmills that won't spin outside of a force niner' and collect newspapers in a great diesel powered lorry staffed by a dozen hairy dustmen all of whom have driven to work in their motor cars.

Environmentalism exists to tax and control in the same way as communism did and does. It seeks to reduce the gap between haves and have nots in the same way as communism did and does.

This *is* achieved, but not by letting the have nots have; but in ensuring that the haves now have not.

It doesn't matter what level of servitude and penury we end up with as long as we are all there together and nobody is doing better than anybody else. Except the authorities of course, but then they deserve their little luxuries considering all they do for us.

And so we continue on our weary way with each new leader continuing the undoing of the nation, holding our hands and whispering sweet nothings in our ears whilst draining the lifeblood from our veins.

Is it really too late for sanity and pride to return to a once great people. I fear that it is but still wistfully hope for salvation. Where is our Cobbett or our Drake? Legend has it that Drake will return to save England in her hour of greatest need. So where the hell is he?

TEN

TEA PARTY PARTY

Good for you, you have a heart, you can be a liberal. Now, couple your heart with your brain, and you can be a conservative.

Glenn Beck-US commentator

A rather startling effect of President Obama's policies has been the inspiration of a virtual uprising across Middle America which has shocked the establishment, Democrat and Republican alike. Whether the Tea Party represents a true peasants revolt or whether it is simply a collection of nut jobs and fruitcakes is almost irrelevant. Nobody (especially a President) wants to see the election of people whose primary attribute seems to be that they hate you. Mr Obama has responded with a reshuffle of his economic advisors but to actually change direction at this point would likely destroy his now fragile creditability. Should we see further Republican triumphs, Obama may well find himself marooned in the White House with little opportunity to recover his declining popularity. The President's antipathy towards the Tea Party is obvious and logical although you might have reasonably assumed that a movement named for an anti-British act of revolution may inspire some sympathy in one with such obvious anti-British feelings. For my part, I can forgive the Yankees for beating us at war but throwing an Englishman's tea overboard was unforgivably spiteful.

The Tea Party is nothing if not a phenomenon. It has terrified the American political establishment which if it achieves nothing else should provide the party's founders with a guaranteed place in heaven. The Tea Partiers have already rocked Washington to its core and changed the political agenda. Whether or not you support its aims is unimportant, it has re-energised the political debate and process and broken the all too cosy atmosphere in the US capital.

For us, an important strand of Obama's persona is his obvious antipathy towards the British. This distaste was demonstrated in the aftermath of the oil spill in the Gulf of Mexico. His hostility towards us was made clear and, at the very least, encouraged the wave of abuse thrown in our direction. BP's chief executive was subjected to a Congressional hearing with a Nuremburg twist and his duties post the spill seemed to consist of life as a red coated Aunt Sally until the oil was cleared and then to go away and not come back. He had to be contrite, miserable and submissive and it was a pity he was not Japanese as he could have just skewered himself live on CBS and allowed the rest of us to move on.

Certainly the attitude of many US politicians bordered on the hysterical in their willingness to bash the Brits. The American public were understandably aggrieved but I do feel that their President stands accused of whipping up anti-British sentiment in order to deflect attention from his and his country's own, not insubstantial culpability in the matter. I understand his political reasons for doing so but it did begin to grate a little. One or two of our politicos took some umbrage and Obama did seem to backtrack somewhat but we have certainly seen that the President is not overwhelmed with love for us. Some say that this lack of appropriate affection has its roots in our alleged 'interrogation' of his Kenyan grandfather in the 1950's. The Obamas' amazing journey from the Mau Mau to the White House would have seemed unlikely to our servicemen in 1958. Then again, it is probably true that banging up the Presidents grandfather was (with the benefit of hindsight) an unfortunate error of judgement on our part.

The election of the first black President was hailed as a milestone in the fight against racism in America. This is dishonest. Obama did not win his election despite racism but rather because of it. The percentage of black voters who voted for him was in the high nineties, can we rationally believe that such a high percentage of any ethnic group would all have agreed with any politicians policies over any opponent? I don't believe that we can, African Americans elected a man because of his skin colour whilst any white man who professed to do so would be condemned as a fascist, Nazi, blah, blah, blah.

The fact that Obama has a very dubious background and surrounds himself with religious cranks, revolutionaries and communists is not sufficient to lessen his allure amongst virtually all blacks and liberal whites. He is a black man and is, therefore, a good thing. My objection to his election is not that a black man became President but that a man became President because he was black. His Presidency does not show that racism is dead but rather that it is very much alive and exists amongst all the peoples of the world.

What the Americans do in their own country is a matter for them. However, no Briton can claim to be vigilant as to his own nation's fortunes without keeping an eye on the other side of the pond. The demographics of the United States are changing as fast, if not faster than they are here. The bond between our nations was based on our historic ties of blood, culture and history. This bond is melting away like April snows. It won't exist at all at some point and we cannot expect the Americans of the future to give a damn about us, let alone grant us the odd favour. This is yet another reason for us to re-discover some concept of independence of mind and spirit. We must have freedom of action or inaction as it suits us.

The Americans sent us the big band which was nice. They also sent us 'rap' which was not. They sent us the celebrity culture which has culminated in Katie Price so they can have that back. They have sent us peanut butter which is okay but they have also sent us 'dunkin donuts' which make us fat and stupid. The jury is out.

This would seem an opportune moment to introduce another old friend, an American this time.

ELEVEN

LONDON ON ENGLAND

One cannot violate the promptings of one's nature without having that nature recoil upon itself.

Jack London

In the early part of the twentieth century, Jack London was renowned in the English speaking world as the foremost name in modern American literature. Though his fame has diminished, his work remains freely available and widely read and there is much in London's tales and studies to entertain, educate and enlighten the Englishman. Numerous biographies of London exist and many editions of his works are accompanied by biographical introductions of this most fascinating man. The picture they tend to paint is that of the socialist, committed to the commonwealth of man and the egalitarian brotherhood. They sweep London's assertations of patriotism and tribal identity aside, assuring the reader that these were merely irritating flaws in his psychological makeup or purely functions of a less enlightened age, environmentally engineered no doubt. He is forgiven his errors notwithstanding that the man would have been bloody furious to be 'forgiven' for opinions which epitomised his very outlook on life.

London's own story is of itself one of great richness. Born into desperate poverty, he made an early conscious decision to rid himself of it. Before the age of 21 he had worked a dozen or more trades; laundryman, tramp, Klondike miner and oyster pirate to name but a few. No matter what he turned his hand to, London experienced success but he knew that sellers of muscle had short careers and thus elected to become a seller of brains.

Beginning his writing career, London found that his harsh exposure to life's realities and his self-education enabled him to bring a fresh, modern style to the flowery 'all American' literature of his day. Romance was sacrificed for realism and his gritty, no nonsense tales became immensely popular with the 'common' people. His own adventures had stood him in good stead, it was clear that his books were researched in Alaskan mining towns and on the swell of the South Seas. London had lived his tales of wonder.

The bare facts declare that London was a member of the radical American Socialist Labour Party for many years, he vehemently opposed the excesses of the American economic system and he quoted Marx regularly on his worldwide lecture tours. Yet this is only the side that the left prefer to project of London. In reality he was something altogether different.

His admitted commitment to radical socialism was borne of his burning sense of outrage at the treatment inflicted on America's poor. He (often reluctantly) adopted the dogma of the left as the only apparent answer to the horrendous conditions endured by America's poorest citizens. When we remember the excesses of the industrialists of that time and the lack of protection for the poor, it was inevitable that London's keen sense of injustice would be stirred. Indeed, London's 'socialism' is today accepted as the political norm or at least thought to be desirable by mainstream politicians.

It is clear from his great social commentaries that London ultimately rejected the Marxist equality myth. Equality of opportunity, rather than of wealth was London's wish and this desire set him apart from, and placed him in conflict with, many of his socialist comrades. His novels are imbued with tales of great individualistic heroism, both human and otherwise and his sociological works, whilst condemning the excesses of a rampantly exploitative capitalism did not simply bemoan the fate of the oppressed but rather applauded the efforts and enterprise of those who strode against the odds to better themselves. Through his writings, London constantly urged his countrymen to improve their own lot rather than wait for some promised but distant revolution to save them.

In 'The Valley of the Moon' (1913) London's courting couple are first encountered as dirt poor city wage slaves whose idea of freedom amounted to a few stolen hours away from their drudgery. London bestows upon them the genes of the first settlers and takes his lovers out of the city's hell and into the countryside, both to regain their heritage and to promise a future for their children. It was no accident that London timed their flight to coincide with a general labour strike thus infuriating his leftist colleagues. London's persistent use of heroic Anglo Saxon characters was a constant irritant to his internationalist friends.

It was perhaps inevitable that such unlikely bedfellows as London and Marx would part company. The irreconcilable conflict between the writer and his Marxist comrades was London's inability to reconcile his socialism with his passionately held nationalism. From his first embrace of the labour movement he had never managed to accept its doctrine of universal equality and multiracialism. It clashed totally with his fierce pride in, and love for, his own people. London would often state that;

'I am a white man first and only then a socialist'.

This thinking, which was so abhorrent to the left both then and far more so now, led London to resist the notion of the equality of nations and man so beloved of his comrades. Inevitably, London would finally resign from the party he had supported for twenty years; his parting shot to that movement was a warning that retains much pertinence today.

'My final word is that liberty, freedom and independence are royal things that cannot be presented to nor thrust upon race and class. If races and classes cannot rise up and by their own strength of brain and brawn, wrest from the world liberty, freedom and independence, they never in time can come to these royal possessions... and if such royal things are kindly presented to them by superior individuals, on silver platters, they will not know what to do with them, will fail to make use of them, and will be what they have always been in the past...inferior races and classes.'

This was always London's position although the left simply chose to ignore this fundamental tenet in one so useful to their cause. London was a theoretical socialist, when dealing with hypothetical situations he stood with the left; yet in his work, when placing his creations in harsh surroundings he would inoculate them with healthy doses of self preservation and independence of spirit and mind.

His classic dog stories, 'Call of the Wild' (1903) and 'White Fang' (1906) owe more to London's belief in evolutionary Darwinism than socialistic tenderness. He yearned for a world in which men and nations could behave kindly and charitably but he understood instinctively that men and nations must fight for their right to be good. To the horror of his pacifist colleagues London supported Britain from the very outset of the Great War.

'War is a silly thing for a rational, civilised man to contemplate...but rational men can't be expected to settle problems in a rational way when others insist on doing it by violent means.'

London never gave up his belief that his own people were special, that they possessed a great destiny. His belief in universal brotherhood crumbled over the years as it collided with reality until he reached his final position on the matter.

... 'there is a certain integrity, a sternness of conscience, a melancholy responsibility which is ours, indutibly ours and which we cannot teach to the oriental as we would teach logarithms or the trajectory of projectiles.'

As can be seen from his allegiance during the Great War, London's pride in his heritage and love of his people produced in him a great affection for England and its population. A visit in 1902 produced perhaps his greatest sociological work, his study of the appalling conditions in the East End, 'The People of the Abyss'. This ground breaking book was researched in the author's usual fashion. He acquired a suit of rags and hurled himself into the hellish world of the city's poorest quarter to encounter his subject first hand. What he discovered shocked even one who had himself endured appalling poverty. This book (which you must read) was just one of a huge number of contemporary East End studies. London's however, is by far the best, being not simply a collection of statistics and an examination of these but rather a vivid portrayal of life and people that retains the power to move to this day.

The book hit British sensibilities squarely on the jaw, the fact that East End conditions were not noticeably improved due only to the lack of political will amongst the nations rulers. It did however, have a huge impact on a younger generation of reformers who would come to power and prominence later.

'The People of the Abyss' was unique in its time in that it was written in an unapologetically journalistic style. Whilst London was careful to include relevant data, his work differed to other contemporary studies of East End life in that these tended to be bookish reports and studies. London's work however, was a passionate condemnation of his findings. London was incapable of simply gathering and reporting facts. He did not stand back and observe but rather launched himself into the 'pit' and thereby gained a more personal view on the situation. He *became* the poor and oppressed. He wrote the complete manuscript while he was in England altering virtually nothing from the first drafts so that his book was almost like a personal diary. He merely slotted in some statistics here and there to illustrate and confirm his experiences and findings.

In addition to London's descriptions of squalor in the world's greatest city he proceeded to set about the mismanagement and misgovernment that was afflicting not just England but the whole Western world. He railed against the waste of resources and people; he (again to the dismay of his fellow socialists) abhorred the policy of equipping third world nations with manufacturing machinery. He warned of shrinking markets and predicted the dumping of goods by affected western nations, this being a horribly accurate vision of the wasteful trade agreements that we find ourselves locked into today.

In perhaps his finest political novel, 'The Iron Heel' (1907), London told of the struggle of the people against the increasingly dictatorial and ultimately triumphant powers of an oligarchy. This fictitious struggle is often considered a prediction of the rise of a worldwide fascist dictatorship. For us in the modern day, 'The Iron Heel' can be seen as a damning indictment of any system which deprives people of freedoms so richly earned. An indictment which can easily be applied to an age where patriotism and love of one's country are so corrupted and despised by society and government.

For Jack London himself, the plight of his people, his own 'melancholy responsibilities' and his increasing health problems began to weigh upon him too heavily during the winter of 1916. He had built a huge ranch which had become his own 'Valley of the Moon' and it was to here that he finally retreated. A drink problem and a bad diet had ruined his once awesome physique and during a particularly painful bout of illness, he overdosed on morphine. Most who knew him believed that it was a deliberate act. And so at the age of forty, Jack London passed into history. His work, however, remains fresh to this day and has retained much of its pertinence.

For the patriot, whether American or English, his best novels remain uplifting and inspirational. His studies remain educational and penetrative. Though much of London's philosophy changed through his life, the one constant was his love of country and people.

There is no comparison between the early twentieth century and the relative poverty of today. The conditions described by London have been thankfully eradicated and hopefully will not return but there still remains the tendency to be more concerned for other peoples rather than our own. We have several million able bodied people without real work, whether voluntarily or otherwise and we have watched as hospitals close across the land. Who remembers John Major's magnanimous gesture to the (then) new South Africa led by Mandela? This consisted of a £1billion interest free, non returnable 'loan' and an additional £1billion 'gift' to help build the new utopia.

Here is the problem; Major led a government that closed, for example, the emergency department of the great St Bartholomew's hospital in the City of London. Unless Major actually enjoyed endangering the lives of City workers, we can assume that the closure was a cost-saving measure. OK, fine, if we're strapped then we have to make sacrifices. But for our leader to then turn around and give £2billion to another people is sickening. Of course, you may say that the gift would help trade but we all know that this is not why he did it. It was a political act engineered to endear him to pro Mandela voters here, one designed to increase his own popularity. Every Prime Minister does this; Cameron recently gave £500m to Pakistan to make up for some things he said that they didn't particularly like. This gift was in addition to the several billion Pounds that we already part with each year and that we have to borrow from the bond market to provide.

Whatever their motivations, there is one undeniable reason why both men should have kept their hands in their pockets. This is simply that although they have done pretty well for themselves, they don't have that kind of lolly lying around indoors. They may be great humanitarians and extremely personally generous but they don't have the wherewithal to bandy billions of quids around like loose change. It is, of course, *our* money and surprisingly or not, most of us who elect governments do so in the (admittedly naive) expectation that they might look after *our* interests. They may have felt their acts were acts of charity but there is a word for spending other people's money and charity it is not.

So why is Jack London included here? After all, he was an American and has been dead for almost a century. The answer is simply that London, all those years ago, put his finger on what is wrong with England and what has been wrong with her for a very long time. *England neglects her own people.* She, by turns, uses and ignores them. She favours others over her own. She can sail the high seas looking to stamp out slavery and yet happily force harsh and dangerous labour on her own little girls. She can destroy a generation of her youth in order to pursue intellectual aims and she can look to build a glorious empire yet allow her own people to live and die in abysmal poverty. She can force her own children from their home towns so that immigrants may have home towns. She can allow the propagation of disgusting ideologies in the name of free speech but condemn and incarcerate those of her own people brave enough to oppose these ideologies.

Jack London would have been appalled to see the condition of England's towns and cities today. The squalor and the shabbiness of them are irrefutable evidence of the carelessness and mismanagement of our political class. A plague on all their houses.

TWELVE

THE GREAT TAX SWINDLE

We contend that for a nation to try to tax itself into prosperity is like a man standing in a bucket and trying to lift himself up by the handle.

Sir Winston Churchill

The Coalition has delivered on its commitment to substantially raise the income tax allowance and this is a perfectly sensible measure. There has been a compensatory tax grab on middle earners but at least the increase in allowance is moving in the right direction for the low paid. Low paid individuals and families likely see their taxes returned to them in the form of benefits. It is symbolic of the crazed nature of our welfare system for the State to take with one hand and to give with the other, not to mention the cost of administering the exchange. I would consider it a conservative ideal to allow people to keep more of their own money. I am all for a far higher allowance that that proposed as I suspect that much of the cost could be recouped by a corresponding scaling back of benefits, tax credits etc. We shall see.

However, just think about the taxes that you do pay, not just the ones that are lifted from your pay packet but all the other too numerous to mention ones that are hidden from your casual gaze. Income tax and National Insurance account for around one third of pay for a basic rate tax payer and more than half for someone in the highest band. In addition, your firm will have to pay employers NI at 14% which, although you do not directly cough it up yourself, is a cost to the business which will be factored into the wages offered you. As a consequence, even a supposedly basic rate taxpayer will see the best part of 50% of his 'salary' disappear in income taxation.

You pick up your wages having paid your share and you decide to celebrate by driving to the seaside. You fill up your tank, Christ! That hurt! These oil barons are having a laugh aren't they? Actually no, Shell is charging you around 50p a litre for that. That company has to buy the rights to it, explore for it, drill for it, ship it, refine it and deliver it to a filling station near you. They have to employ people to take your money and to sell you the Mars bar that you pick up by the till. At the time of writing, Shell charges less than the price of the chocolate for this service. It delivers useable gasoline, drawn from the bowels of the earth in some of the most inhospitable God-forsaken holes in the world for around ten bob a go. This company employs tens of thousands of Britons, pays billions of Pounds in British taxes and billions more into British pension and savings funds by way of share dividends.

So why do you feel so queasy when filling up your car? Ah yes, the taxman. Tax on petrol amounts to something around 190% of the value of the fuel itself. Read that again, 190%! What is even more galling is that part of this percentage is V.A.T. This is particularly pernicious. The Government levies V.A.T. on the whole price of a litre of petrol, including the fuel duty itself.

V.A.T. on tax! We should be crashing our Vauxhall Vivas through the gates of Parliament as we speak. What if the Treasury applied V.A.T. to income tax thus increasing your burden by a further 20%? Would you accept that? No? I can't see the difference personally.

Anyway, you have reached the seaside and fancy a pint. Tax! Smoke a cigarette? Tax! Buy your family a meal? Tax! Bunch of flowers for the wife? Tax! Take copious breaths of sea air? Well, soon perhaps, they already tax your light, your heat and much of your food so why not the air that you breathe? In fact, as we are to be taxed in order to provide 'clean' air I think that we may have already reached a point beyond satire.

Oh, and when you die, they'll have another 40% of what's left, thank you very much.

Indeed, taxes on capital need to be factored in too. A year or three ago, there was something of a fuss regarding the private equity barons and their contribution to the Exchequer. Outrage at tax rates of 10% on capital gains was affected by many Labour MPs who suggested that such people were cheating the system. Here, the public was only being fed part of the whole story. The insinuation was that the private equity people were breaking the rules. This was more than a little misleading, for as far as one can tell, the full and correct rates of tax were being collected in accordance with the rules. The Business Asset Scheme which demanded only one tenth of profits to be paid away was a relatively new innovation introduced by Gordon Brown whilst at number 11. The scheme applied to all who owned shares in their own business or in their employer. I happened to think that the scheme was a little open to abuse and I certainly did not favour the overly indulgent treatment of people who make vast amounts of money. However, The BAS was a Labour introduction and it seemed a little rich for Labour MPs to pillory people for complying with Government policy.

Notwithstanding the above, taxes on capital have a woeful effect on the economic well being of the country. Small fortunes are frittered away, hidden, or expatriated in order to avoid Inheritance Tax. Huge sums are tied up in investment accounts paralysed by Capital Gains Tax rules. These monies represent capital that could and should be funding industry, enterprise and employment. CGT and IHT cause real damage to every tier of society and we should be rid of them at the earliest possible moment. Of course, complete abolition (of CGT in particular) is unlikely. Accepting this, a future Chancellor could consider some form of amnesty, perhaps offering investors a short period in which to restructure portfolios thus releasing capital for investment elsewhere. There would be much detail to work through but such an amnesty would certainly be a boon for markets and therefore pension funds. This boost to savings might well save the state a great deal of money in the long term.

There have been numerous efforts to re-jig the CGT system and Gordon Brown alone had at least two stabs at it. Whilst headlines were duly grabbed, we should remember that Brown's final set of new rules were a knee jerk reaction to the private equity furore mentioned earlier and gave the distinct impression of being knocked up over a quick pint in a hurried attempt to regain the political initiative. Certainly it seemed that Brown captured an extra portion of the loot generated by the private equity barons largely to garner positive headlines in the mainstream press. I was not against higher taxes for these individuals per se, certainly as I staggered under my own tax burden. However, the proposals (doing away with indexation and taper relief and replacing them with a flat tax) seemed rather at odds with the Government's ten year drive to encourage long term share ownership. It was all very strange, more than a little hurried and indicated panic. It certainly seemed odd to change the entire CGT system for the whole country just to satisfy demands to increase taxation for a group numbering a few hundred people.

The fact is that a Pound generated by a business endures National Insurance on any wages that it pays, V.A.T. on any supplies and services that it needs and Corporation tax on any profit that it manages to make. This Pound is also subject to personal taxes on the proportion it pays away to staff. Any remaining value that is paid to shareholders is subject

110

to the taxes falling due on dividends. Any pennies left to you are subject to vehicle duty, fuel duty, tobacco and alcohol duties, V.A.T., council taxes, airline taxes, insurance taxes, energy taxes, taxes on your water, clothing and pretty much anything else you can think of. Of every Pound generated in this country, the state ends up claiming the vast majority of it.

This is absolutely fine, as in return we have world class hospitals, roads with no holes, an immaculate public transport system, enough policemen and well equipped armed forces large enough to cope with our love of a good war. We have the best schools in the world, the highest quality of care for our elderly and a university system producing an unlimited supply of brilliant people to service our world beating design, technology and manufacturing industries. They're worth every brass farthing I'd say.

How can the state take so much from us and still be bankrupt? How can it extract the lion's share of the product of a rich nation and still manage to provide such woefully inadequate services as it does? The answer lies predominately in a cancer that has been growing for a hundred years but which has become progressively more virulent over recent decades.

The welfare state is amongst the most difficult of topics with which to hold a rational conversation. It raises great passion, whether it be genuine or simply designed to prevent any reasonable discourse. The original concept and implementation were welcomed as a major step forward for the working classes and their families although the original aim of 'cradle to grave' cover promised a utopia which was always likely to disappoint.

The original aims have been twisted over the years until we have reached the point where the system is hideously unaffordable, damaging to the character of the nation and providing a level of service which is appallingly poor as a return on our investment.

Unemployment benefits are only necessary in a system that produces unemployment as an essential part of that system. Certainly there are those who find themselves workless through no fault of their own but even here, the system can be damaging. We have all seen, probably at first hand, the morale sapping effects of the benefits culture.

I once had a very good friend who managed to impregnate his girlfriend at a relatively young age. The local Council responded to his indiscretion by first ignoring the new little family and then, eventually, placing it on the fourteenth floor of a particularly grimy tower block. Each day, my friend would rise early and travel across town to the small printing business where he worked and trained for greater things. What with the rent, rates and the babe, things were very tight financially but my friend persevered as, once qualified, life would surely become easier. Actually, things were to become easier rather sooner than expected. Disaster struck. Well, actually it became a disaster but began as a small blip, what should have been an inconvenient interlude in a life of improvement and progression.

The small business ran into some difficulties due, as I recall, to the profligacy of one of the partners. The firm stopped trading but the second partner assured my friend that a new business would rise from the ashes within three months and that there would be a guaranteed place for the young apprentice. However, it did mean a layoff and the young man found himself at the unemployment office for the first time in his life. To his great surprise, he found that his financial circumstances did not decline. Indeed, with rent paid, no work related expenses and cash for his partner and child, he actually found himself rather better off

112

than he had been before. I still recall sharing his bemusement at such a curious turn of events.

Shortly afterwards, a chance conversation in the pub led to short term employment labouring on a local building site. The wages offered were poor but with no taxes due and allied to the benefits now filling his pot, this low grade employment made a startling difference to the family finances. My friend now found himself in a position of relative affluence which he had never experienced before. He even took his little family on a holiday which would have been unthinkable a few weeks before.

True to his word, partner number two came good and a new printing business emerged with a vacancy for an ambitious young apprentice. By this point however, it was clear that accepting this job offer would impoverish my friend to a very real extent. He did think it over but not for very long. The baby needed things and his partner had gotten used to having money in her purse. What my friend did was illegal but no more so than was the case with countless people around him. It was immoral but no more so than the immoral system that allowed such situations to develop. The family thus lived off the State and with each passing year the chances of escaping the benefits trap decreased.

My friend was a bright young man once, one who looked forward to a better future. I don't see much of him these days. He still lives in that tower block and, if I'm honest, is pretty miserable company. It is a great pity, another incidence of a decent soul corrupted by the welfare state and three lives ruined.

Some would have you believe that the 'benefit cheat' is somewhat of a myth, or at least a reality which has been wildly exaggerated. The sentiment is that whilst we all enjoy the Daily Mail's exposé of the wheelchair bound claimant who doubles as the Big Bopper at the weekends, such things are uncommon and incidental in the grand scheme of things. They are not. I grew up in an area where working whilst claiming was a widely embraced way of life. As described above, a minor accident or a short term layoff was often sufficient to embed a man in the benefits system and keep him there indefinitely. The dishonesty of it all was barely considered and was accepted as a legitimate method of providing for the family. The attitude was, and is, that the only one being cheated was the government and to hell with them.

> No working person should ever receive a penny less than even the most deserving of benefit claimants, the very moment that it was possible to do so was the moment that the welfare system tipped over into unsustainability. To receive less for work, any work, than it is possible to receive doing none is tantamount to a sin against nature and will encourage not only slothfulness but also inevitable friction amongst the population.

George Osborne was right to say that it is wrong for the worker to be up and out before the winter's dawn whilst his neighbour turns over dreaming of his state sponsored breakfast. For two members of the same tribe to lead such an unbalanced co-existence is only likely to further divide the tribe itself.

Of course there is genuine unemployment, particularly outside of the south east. This is certainly a matter for the Government. The destruction of our industries may have seemed inevitable at the time but only due the old British conditions of bad management, state meddling and intransigence on the part of the workforce and their unions.

Do the Germans not still have a successful manufacturing sector? Do the French not still manufacture their own motor cars? Do the Italians not still produce world class clothing? So how is it that we cannot do so in any meaningful way? The answer lies in our own stupidity and the old, old tendency to strive for the cheapest available option, to *make do*. We would have struggled to produce cheap motor cars when faced with the new Asian competition but this does not mean we couldn't have used our inventiveness to produce higher margin vehicles. Our clothing industry could not compete with the cheap labour of the East but this does not mean that we could not have gravitated to the higher quality markets that are in fact more profitable anyway. It is this obsession with cheapness that is our undoing. It has taken a manufacturing industry that was the envy of the world and reduced it to a shell.

How is it rational to keep millions of people on benefits and suck in cheap labour to take their places? Apart from the hideous expense, the social problems allied to unemployment are obvious to all who wish to see and progressively even to those who do not. Then, unbelievably, you have the left bemoaning the fact that our cheap imported labour is being exploited and underpaid which rather spectacularly misses the point of it.

And what do we get in return? Our food is gathered cheaply enough that the supermarkets can offer you a reasonable deal. You can have your car cleaned for a fiver and (apparently) get someone to fix your leaky tap for a reasonable sum.

And what is the downside? You get millions of able bodied men and their dependents sitting around doing nothing. You get millions of foreigners taking their places in the workforce who surprisingly enough all need housing, healthcare, policing and the rest of it. What kind of a bargain do you really think you are getting when you consider the proportion of your own income than ends up in the Chancellors coffers in order to keep the whole sorry ship afloat.

On a recent visit to Norway, I noted the absence of anything resembling an underclass. A small purchase brought me into contact with a shop worker who emphasised my point for me. She was young, presentable (no terrifying hairdo or pieces of scrap iron protruding from her skin) and spoke excellent English. She may have worked a till but she was pleasantly mannered and well educated.

Goods are expensive in Oslo but if these high prices help to maintain a decent income and provide a good education for Norway's shop girls then I would think that the Norwegians' are getting something right that we are getting very wrong. It may cost an arm and a leg to buy cigarettes from a Norwegian shop girl but then it doesn't bankrupt the country to support her either.

THIRTEEN

ISLAM, FELLOW TRAVELLERS AND INTENDED CONSEQUENCES

Believers, make war on the infidels who dwell around you. Deal firmly with them. Know that God is with the righteous.

The Koran

A year or so ago, the French immigration minister called for a general ban on the wearing of burkhas. This law has now passed and we await developments. A contributor to the Daily Mail online debate on the matter wondered if any 'acceptable' politicians in the U.K. will follow suit. It was a feeble question although quite possibly rhetorical. The fact is, no 'acceptable' politician from any 'acceptable' party is ever likely to have the courage to face down the political Islamists who are progressively setting the agenda in our country. Our main parties have selection systems and procedures that make it extremely difficult for men of principal to advance within them. Any worthy soul who does raise his head above the parapet has it shot off very quickly. This is as true for the Tories as it is for the others. Only parties currently considered beyond the pale are attempting to face the Islamic threat. This is a shame and it seems strange to me that we can only 'accept' those politicians who lie to us whilst slithering upon their bellies to their new masters. Why can we not have a politician that we actually agree with?

It is common for writers and commentators to make it plain that although they write in defence of some other party's policy, they actually find the party itself abhorrent. I shall not do that. I am not a thug; actually I am quite a pleasant chap when you get to know me. I am not a

117

moron with a peanut for a brain; actually I have a rather successful career in the City (although I recognise that this probably rates me lower than 'Nazi scum' at the moment). I do not hate, threaten, harass or assault and it is a pity that I would seem to be at such odds with so many of my fellow Englishmen. We are, after all, countrymen and would seem to have at least some common ground. It is my belief that opinion in this country will continue to polarise as our situation deteriorates. I would hope that at some point in the future we might be more united in the defence of our civilisation. If we are not, we shall simply not survive as a people and our differences will be meaningless.

It is, of course, true that the majority of Muslims in Britain do not support Islamic terrorism. At least I believe it to be true. It is also (probably) true that they do not particularly advocate an Islamic state, Sharia law etc. This may be comforting but is largely irrelevant. It would not take a majority of any group or sect to usurp a weak and spineless British state. The history of the world is strewn with examples of dedicated and committed minorities asserting themselves over complacent majorities. The Bolshevik ascent in 1917 is the classic example.

It is desperately important for us to regain our European Christian identity and it is equally vital that we do so quickly. Our problem is how to do so. It is difficult to imagine even the faintest stirrings of such a renaissance emerging from our present political class. To recover, we need politicians and political parties that will dispense with political correctness and address our many problems from a purely pragmatic perspective. Whomsoever dares to do this will attract a storm of condemnation at least equal to the experience of Nick Griffin and his followers. Any movement originating from the middle classes will surely hesitate and back peddle as Middle England is unlikely to be able to cope with the bile, hatred and violence that will be heaped upon it as soon as any real dissent is shown. As this is evident, we can rest assured that our decline will continue and hasten. We will be left with only the 'something' which our gentlefolk currently find unpalatable. One day, all that will remain will be to decide which side of the fence you wish to stand. Sitting upon it will not be an option.

The politics of Tower Hamlets are of particular interest, not necessarily because they are any more extreme or outrageous than that of other inner city areas (although they may well be so) but because they are carried on within a brief stroll of the City of London and that of Westminster. For the outrages that occur there to have been ignored by the great and the good in their London palaces and gentlemen's clubs is a supreme feat of ignorance, cowardice and defeatism.

The East End has always been highly politicised, it was an incubator of the Labour movement and of many other radical groups from Mosley's British Union of Fascists to the Workers Revolutionary Party. It has also always been a magnet for the 'committed' middle classes to go and try out whatever idiocy they have been exposed to in our universities before taking that job with Daddy and returning home to marry Jemima. They would come in their patronising thousands and they would tell us where we were going wrong, how we were mistaken in our thinking and how we should comport ourselves in order to receive their patronage and praise.

They told us for years not to be beastly to the newcomers of the post war period, that we should welcome them with open arms and of how we could learn so much from them. We were replaced in the affections of the philanthropic by new people seen as rather more worthy of indulgence. Old toys discarded for new.

We heard continuously of minority rights, of how the perturbed majority should not be permitted to impose its will upon vulnerable minority groups. We heard this repeatedly until some point in the 1990's when the 'white British' population of the borough finally declined to minority status. Then, funnily enough, something changed. We learnt that 'democracy' must out, that 'democracy' required that the interests of the majority must be pursued and respected and that 'minority' views would be treated as such.

This kind of thing came to a head in the local council elections of 1993. A few months previously, a council by election had resulted in the election of a councillor representing the British National Party, an event that sent shockwaves through the country. In 1993, all council seats were up for grabs and there was a threat that the BNP might make further gains which would have been most unwelcome, democracy or no. The people of Tower Hamlets witnessed one of the greatest, if not *the* greatest mobilisation of a major party machine outside of a general election. Huge numbers of Labour activists were drawn into the area and the particular focus was in ensuring the complete and total utilisation of the Asian vote. Social workers, interpreters and 'community leaders' were conscripted to ensure that every last Asian vote contributed to Labour's recovery of the lost seat and the retention of any other others that were vulnerable.

This was fine, well if not fine it was within the rules, political parties are allowed to do this. What was not fine at all was the accompanying disregard for the sanctity of the electoral process, the violation of the secret ballot and the rank violence and intimidation employed during that campaign. You didn't have to be involved in the election; just living in the borough during that time was a revelation to anyone with eyes and ears.

Firstly, many votes were cast by people who did not reside in the borough, or who didn't exist at all. These voted were merrily counted.

Secondly, several people (to my knowledge) were arrested for personation (attempting to cast more than one vote). No charges were brought.

Thirdly, and most outrageously, the secrecy of the previous election was violated in a criminal effort to intimidate certain sections of the BNP 'protest' vote. This is actually very simple to do if you work in the relevant council department or if you know someone who does. Each ballot paper has a little number printed upon it which corresponds with a person's name on the returning officers list. Subsequent to a poll it is possible to identify the supporters of a particular party or candidate. By this method, you may also deduce whether this supporter was someone you could put the squeeze on or whether you were likely to have him break your arm. Mrs Agnes Oldlady could be leant on whilst Slasher Norris would be best left alone. Thus, elderly and vulnerable BNP voters were targeted and many of them received little visits from Labour activists, mobs of them.

I know that this happened, my own Aunt received a knock at her door from a group of 'delegates' who intimated that they knew where her sympathies had lain in the previous election and that she would do much better if she didn't repeat her error. Granted, she told them to 'bugger off' but many of her generation were suitably perturbed and a climate of fear spread around the day centres. These outrages were reported to the Police who made their little notes and rolled their little eyes.

On Election Day, the BNP councillor at the centre of this storm managed to increase his vote by over 30% and got absolutely trounced. Some observers estimated the turnout in his ward at something between 105% and 115%. On the following day the (Liberal Democrat) Mayor of the borough publicly called for an enquiry into the conduct of the election and made an appeal to the Home Secretary to look into what had occurred just two miles from Westminster. I believe Michael Howard should be responding at some point in the near future.

He who excuses himself accuses himself. **17th Century English proverb**

This was the first occasion that electoral fraud was apparent to me. Since that time, I have heard and read of countless examples of its growing use and abuse and its aiding and abetting almost exclusively by the Labour Party. Whole towns have had their elections rigged or corrupted. The methods are basic but easy to execute. Have you ever entered a polling station a few minutes before closing and found that your name has been crossed out? I have, and it wasn't a little error. They didn't think that I was coming and cast my vote on my behalf, the little darlings.

And what happens at closing time? Everybody has to leave except the workers who have been selected from the council's own workforce, find one that isn't a member of Unison if you can. Our ballot papers are then left at the mercy of these carefully selected officers until some later point when the ballot boxes are removed to another place to be counted. Quite often, the old fashioned sturdy metal boxes have been replaced with ones of plastic or cardboard. Apparently, the metal boxes are too heavy, 'elf 'n safety innit', and now we have shoe boxes that a five year old could open with a spoon. They are sealed but only with those little plastic seals that you can get in B&Q, five for a Pound.

In the latest round of European elections, competing parties were allowed to place their own seals on the boxes as well as the official ones. In many places, these seals mysteriously fell off overnight which was a little puzzling. However the official seals were intact (five for a Pound, you can do it) and so the returning Officers decreed that all was well. The Returning Officers, who work for the council, are members of Unison etc.

I mention this to re-emphasise an earlier point. The leftists will affect commitment to democracy but are only interested in it as far as it furthers their own ends. They will cheat if they have to, willingly and without shame. They will corrupt the democratic process if they believe that it will not deliver their preferred result. Such corruption does not occur everywhere of course, only where it counts.

It remains an odd thing to me that when an East Londoner complains that he has been taken over, he can still, in the face of overwhelming evidence, be met with scorn, derision and quite often, hate-filled condemnation. How can he say such a terrible thing? What an ignorant little Nazi he must be. How can he not appreciate our brave new world? It may prove instructive to look at the facts of the matter rather than listen to the rainbow chasers.

- **Forty years ago, the population of Tower Hamlets was overwhelmingly 'White British'. Now this group is in a distinct minority in the borough (and in many others). Any white skinned person you pass in the street is as likely to be Eastern European as English.**
- **The number of 'White British' councillors is tiny when compared with the numbers of those of Asian extraction.**
- **The demographics of the borough's schools are such that the majority of its schools have only a small number of 'White British' children, or often none at all.**
- **The local council has been infiltrated and controlled by an extremist Islamist group dedicated to the creation of an Islamic state in Britain.**
- **The economic life of the borough has been in the hands of Asian businesses for many years.**

- **Asian activists are responsible for performing acts of vote rigging and other electoral frauds.**

- **There are many no-go areas where a 'White British' (or indeed any other non-Asian) person is very wise not to go. The Rainbow brigade claims that these 'no-go' areas do not exist but as there are many places where people don't go (through fear) I would suggest that they are talking their usual garbage.**

The Whitechapel Mosque (as one example) has been a centre for and propagator of radical Islam and fundamentalism for 25 years. Everyone knew (or at least strongly suspected) what was going on in that place but again any reasoned discussion was quashed for a very long time. It was only when links to extremism and terrorism were proven beyond doubt that any kind of comment was made in the press, not that it made any difference.

This Islamist control has now reached the stage where activists patrol the streets ordering females to cover themselves and instructing males that they ensure that 'their' women do the same. They cut and bludgeon non-Muslim teachers who dare to mention that there are religions other than Islam. How can we allow such things in our capital when we are sending young men and women to their deaths in Afghanistan to stamp them out? Please tell me how?

Take a drive through Stepney or Whitechapel and take a good look around. Stop believing what you are told and start believing the evidence before your eyes. If you can do this and still tell the Cockney that he hasn't been 'taken over', then you will be either mad and delusional or simply lying.

FOURTEEN

HEROD'S LEGACY

I've noticed that everybody that is for abortion has already been born.

Ronald Reagan

The biblical tale of King Herod's slaughter of the innocents is widely taken to be fable. The story's modern day equivalent however is tragically real. Since the dawn of civilisation it has been the policy of nations to protect, by law, their unborn children. In Britain it has been otherwise for only forty five years of our history. These four and half decades are an aberration which future generations may well look upon with horror.

The act of parliament permitting abortion was passed in 1967. It was ostensibly a private members bill forwarded by former Liberal party leader David Steel but one that was openly encouraged and supported by Home Secretary Roy Jenkins and the incumbent Labour government. It was one of three major reform bills of the period seen by the left as reforming and progressive along with those abolishing capital punishment and the decriminalisation of homosexual acts.

The law, as it has stood since 1967 (we shall look at one or two amendments as we go along) permits termination where mother or child face some danger to either physical or mental wellbeing. The loose wording was designed for coaches and their horses to be driven through and practically invited misuse. The bill initially set the limit for termination at 28 weeks, thereby accepting that it was safe and humane to remove a 'foetus' from a seven month pregnant woman. The limit was later reduced to 24 weeks after even the 'pro-choice' lobby became a little perturbed at the constant reports of perfectly formed babies being hacked to pieces.

125

At this moment in time, before the age of 24 weeks an unborn child is not deemed to possess that most fundamental of human rights, the right to life. This is permitted on the premise that prior to the time limit; the foetus is incapable of independent existence and is therefore not an individual human entity but merely a growth inside a woman's body. Of course, a 23 week old foetus *is* incapable of survival without its mother or a surrogate mother, i.e. medical science but then the same can be said for a one or two year old child and indeed for many of the elderly and disabled adults in our country today.

If we were to take a one year old boy to a remote, uninhabited area and abandone him, it is most unlikely that he could live for more than a few days. He simply could not survive without the protection of his mother (or a surrogate). A small child is as incapable of independent survival as is an unborn child. There should be no moral or legal distinction between helpless dependent children based on arithmetic or on what is convenient to us.

The essential problem of the pro life lobby is the great difficulty they face in getting their message across against a huge tide of misinformation and propaganda. Most people simply do not think about abortion very much, rather vaguely accepting it as somehow the norm and perhaps in some cases viewing it as potentially convenient. There has also been a very successful campaign by abortion advocates to silence dissent on the subject. Certainly, it is a brave man who ventures a pro-life view in the company of pro-abortion women.

The questions are there however for anyone willing to ponder them.

A live embryo cannot walk, cannot talk and is incapable of any more than the most basic of movements. Is it then acceptable to discard this soul on the grounds that it is somehow not real, whole or even human?

As we are not generally allowed to kill human beings we might ask ourselves some questions.

- **Is a human foetus human?**
- **If it is alive, is it a live being?**

I would venture that the answer to both questions is clearly affirmative, so how can we not consider this child a human being?

We might also wish to consider the ten year old boy. He cannot compete with an adult's physical power or strength of thought. Indeed, he cannot perform the most fundamental of human functions, that of reproduction. Are we then to accept that our ten year old children are less 'human' than we adults?

Is it then acceptable to bestow lesser rights on a new born baby boy than on a ten year old child on the grounds that he is a less developed creature? No, of course not, the idea is ridiculous and obscene. However we can and do accept that a 24 week old unborn is a human being deserving of care and protection but that one of 23 weeks and 6 days can be cut from the womb and thrown into an incinerator.

The various methods used in terminations are so grotesque that I do not wish to dwell upon them for very long. That said, we are in the business of truth telling so a very brief word on the mechanics of this holocaust is in order.

Caesarean section abortion (hysterotomy) is commonly used with later term terminations. CS abortion is the same as a CS itself until the cord is cut. In CS, the baby's phlegm is sucked out and every effort is made to preserve the child's life. In CSA, the child is dropped into a bucket and left to die. They all move, they all breathe and some even cry. These killings differ in sophistication from Dilation and Curettage (D & C) terminations where the unborn is hacked to pieces whilst still inside the womb. The body parts are sucked out following dismemberment. If an abortionist did this to a newborn baby he would likely find himself in a cell alongside with Hannibal Lecter.

Perhaps the greatest force for, firstly the legalisation of abortion and its continuing and increasing usage has been the insistence of the powerful feminist lobby. This group's policy is, of course, to be differentiated from that of the majority of British women who still choose to carry their babies and who could conceive of nothing more horrific than the killing of their child. It is undeniably true that the debate on abortion that is urgently needed is suppressed by pro abortion groups who scream hysterically at anyone who dares to question their right to kill. They do this, they say, to protect the sanctity of a woman's 'right to choose'. It is ironic that this 'right' when introduced in the 1960's coincided with the advent of efficient and freely available contraceptives. In fact, in today's society the widely available and very highly effective forms of contraception have largely negated the need for the form of post conception contraceptive which termination has largely become.

It is not acceptable for a couple, or a single woman, to waive parental responsibilities on the grounds of bad luck. It is not morally acceptable to terminate the life of a child, a fellow human being because the pregnancy is unwanted or inconvenient. Contraception is the prevention of new life. Abortion is the termination of new life already in existence. There is a huge difference.

The main thrust of the abortionist's argument seems to be that the foetus/embryo/child is 'part' of a woman's body and as such she has the right to dispose of it at will. Let's just look at what they are saying here.

Anyone with the slightest knowledge of human anatomy understands that the essential characteristics of a person are decided at the point of conception. Height, build, sex, colour etc are planned or preprogrammed at this point. At 30 days, the unborn has a brain, eyes, ears, mouth, kidneys, liver and a heart pumping blood which it has made itself. At 8 weeks all body systems are present and at 11 weeks all systems function. The child will sleep, wake and even urinate. By this stage, it can even be taught to respond to sound signals and it recoils from pain. The baby may be tiny but it is still a baby, just as a crumb of bread is still bread.

In light of this, the 'one body' argument looks a tad weak which is why pro-abortionists prefer to quash any discussion on the subject. There is (especially in the private clinics) a tendency to deny pregnant women or protect them from, the full unvarnished truth about the human life that grows inside them. To graphically describe the human condition of the unborn child would likely upset the Mother contemplating or planning a termination and she is likely to be assured that her baby is merely a collection of cells. This is the most dishonest manifestation of society's desire to avoid and ignore the truth about abortion. The mother should be told the complete and absolute truth however painful or upsetting, anyone considering something as drastic as the termination of her child's life should at least be in possession of all the facts.

Something in excess of 200,000 abortions are performed in Britain each year under the guidelines of the Abortion act. Very few are the consequence of emergency procedures allowed for in the wording of the act. Of the rest, the vast and overwhelming majority are procedures attributed to 'the risk of injury to the physical or mental health of the mother'. Here is the legal definition that essentially gives us 'abortion on demand'. Although the law officially denies the existence of such a thing in this country, even rabid pro-abortionists admit and often celebrate that it exists in reality. To contend that the 1967 act does not provide abortion on demand is nonsense. It is bordering on the impossible for a doctor to refuse an abortion request.

Here is the crux of the matter. Do we accept a woman's right to abort her child's life on demand? To provide this 'right' was the motivating pressure behind the 1967 act, other stated motives are designed to mislead. The act was not introduced to provide abortions for victims of rape or those who genuinely faced health risks by carrying full term. Such terminations were catered for before 1967. What was not permitted was the ending of an innocent child's life because the mother simply did not wish for it to continue.

What we also endure today is the proliferation of private clinics providing termination services. Some may point to their relieving effect on the NHS but surely it is a matter of concern to us that private business plays a part in such things. Private clinics exist to make profits and can have little interest in deterring customers. Indeed, as science progresses, there are unlimited business opportunities for the abortion industry. The growth of the stem cell industry should also be of great concern to us. How long before pregnancy and termination is encouraged to order? Breeding and killing of babies is a horrific concept but then we have already accepted the killing part haven't we? If the people are willing to accept the continuing and growing slaughter in hospitals and termination clinics, what on earth won't they accept? The major, moral objection to such a trade has already been overcome in the minds of many, many people. Abortion is overwhelmingly a moral issue. It transcends politics and religion and is still there even if we choose to ignore it.

Imagine a tiny but perfectly formed child, secure in his mother's protection, his life in the world awaiting him. With no warning (or pain relief) he is attacked with sharpened steel. In a few moments he is disturbed and dismembered, he is taken from life and he dies unnamed and unwanted. An inconvenience destined for the furnace.

It is imperative that the truth behind the abortion industry is made known to every man and woman in this country. The 'collection of cells' myth is long overdue for its own termination and every mother contemplating an abortion should be made fully aware of the enormity of what she is considering to do. This is the minimum we should expect in a truly civilised society.

Many pro-lifers have deep Christian faith and are often portrayed as religious cranks. It may be true of some that they believe they are serving God by opposing the abortion business. Then again, believing in God, even today, is not a particularly evil thing to do. Believing you *are* God however can have some pretty serious consequences. We human beings are not yet worthy of filling our maker's shoes. The conception of a human life is a process that should not be reversible at will. Who among men can possibly decide with a moral certainty when a child is a child and when it is not?

Aside from the moral arguments it is also a matter of tribal survival. If we accept that the post war population has remained reasonably constant and we acknowledge the existence of very large numbers of immigrants within our shores, then it follows that our own numbers have been lessened in direct relation to the number of immigrants here. By even the lowest estimates, this is a huge number and an unsustainable one. Every time you see a non Briton, he is not there in addition to but in place of one of your own people. Remember that. We are literally committing suicide. And murder.

FIFTEEN

NOOSE SURRENDER

Capital punishment is our society's recognition of the sanctity of human life.

Orrin Hatch-U S Senator

Since the abolition of capital punishment in Britain a large majority of Britons have consistently expressed a desire for its return. Despite the unarguable desire on the part of the people for the death penalty, Parliament has consistently voted against its reinstatement. Our elected representatives have ignored the wishes of the public for decades. Why? The simple and stock answer is that this issue (unlike most other policy) is a matter of conscience and as a majority of MPs oppose the death penalty, well that's that! Of course the man in the street cannot (at least with absolute surety) claim to be the superior of the MP. But, by the same token, can a few hundred men and women claim such superiority over a whole nation?

I would like to venture that many who oppose the majority wish on this issue often misunderstand the true case for it. Actually, many of those who support capital punishment also fail to comprehend it. Though the experiences of other nations (notably Asian nations) suggest that capital punishment has a deterrent effect in regard to certain crimes (where would you rather smuggle heroin, Thailand or Teignmouth?) there is no concrete evidence supporting a similar link in cases of murder and what evidence does exist is challenged. It is quite possible that a deterrent effect would be impossible to prove one way or another. I am perfectly willing to accept this on the grounds that it simply doesn't matter. It is ultimately irrelevant. The death penalty is what it says on the tin. It is not the death deterrent; it is a penalty, and a penance to be paid after the wilful taking of a life. If such a penalty has a deterrent effect then all well and good.

Let's take a simple (and unashamedly emotive) example.

If a man deliberately kills a child, we have the following situation;

- **An innocent child who is dead.**

- **The killer of this child who is alive.**

There is obviously something wrong here. If we do not exact retribution for our child's murder there is a tacit acceptance that the child has less of a right to life than does his killer. The State is recognising the right to life of a vicious child murderer while the life of the child has ended. In effect; our society now recognises that we may take a child's life without endangering our own. This is the reality and no amount of waffle and cant will alter the fact. I suppose that even the most disturbed liberal would acknowledge that the victim's life is *as* important as that of the murderer but the State no longer acknowledges this except with worthless platitudes.

The whole point of justice is implied in its very name. The law must be just. It must be fair and equitable. If you steal a television the punishment must be somehow proportionate to the crime. This proportionality is the key to a successful justice system, one that can be respected by the people. We should not lock up jaywalkers for life and we should not give community service to armed robbers.

If you carry out the deliberate killing of a child the same standard should apply. Many of those who oppose the death penalty admit that if the victim was a close relative they might well feel differently. The relatives of victims can be forgiven for willing death to the killer and everyone sympathises. The State has removed our individual right to extract natural justice and it should therefore be courageous enough to implement such justice on our behalf.

I accept that a small group should govern the lives of the bewildered herd. My own experience is that few people care passionately about politics or government and fewer still understand them. I don't accept however that the 'elite' should therefore please themselves and ignore the *desires* of the people. I stress desires because I believe that the key to good government, in Britain anyway, is for the British people's instincts and wishes to be articulated and legislated for by the nation's most able people.

MPs should not only formulate and improve policy but also accept the wishes of the people and strive to find the best ways of satisfying them. An MP must have freedom of movement but where a vast and overwhelming majority of citizens over a time span of decades desire the implementation of a particular policy (i.e. the return of the death penalty for those who murder our children) then it is really not too much to ask of a democracy to grant that wish.

A large majority of people would like to see the return of the death penalty for child murderers. This is a wish that transcends political allegiances. Like other burning issues, immigration for example, the wishes of the people are similar across a broad spectrum. Unfortunately these wishes are not reflected in policy formulated by the three, predominantly liberal main parties. Any party that took its commitment to the extreme of actually giving the people what they want would likely clean up.

SIXTEEN

THE ECONOMIC CRISIS

There are two kinds of economist, those that don't know, and those who don't know they don't know.

JK Galbraith

At the start of the 'crisis' we were invited to believe that deflation is the long term threat to our prosperity. We were given to understand that the economic measures employed around the world were deployed in order to combat this deflation, at least in part. This is extremely convenient as it does rather free things up for governments to continue their lunatic spending orgies.

The 200 year old national debt continues its inexorable rise. Before the latest crisis hit home, many believed that at approximately 42 % of GDP, the debt was not a major issue. Now sitting at in excess of 70% of GDP it most certainly is. A report from credit ratings agency S&P pointed to a debt ratio of 169% by 2050 unless we see *further adjustment either to current fiscal stance or to social healthcare costs'*. I would seriously doubt that UK sovereign debt would retain its AAA rating with a national debt of something approaching 200% of GDP. The prospect of Gilts rated as speculative or 'junk' bonds may make investors think twice at supporting the Government's 50 year issues.

It is a convoluted route from the family's shopping basket to the financial affairs of the world's great nations. That said, there is at least an interesting comparison to be made. Very few individuals truly believe that they can become wealthy by spending all their money and by borrowing more in order to spend that too. Why then do governments believe that if all individuals can be encouraged to be profligate then society as a whole can become richer? Such an odd notion can enjoy acceptance for a period as the population consumes heartily but there is an eventual price to pay and we are paying it now. Earnings are falling, taxes are rising and there will be a fall in living standards.

The average US male earns less in real terms than he did in 1971. He may have 'felt' wealthier, certainly before the crisis began to bite but this warm glow of affluence had been achieved by working longer hours, borrowing far more than he would have dared do before (or been permitted to do), and by his wife entering the work place to bolster the family finances.

I use 1971 as a comparison as there are some interesting parallels between then and now. Messrs Nixon, Heath (the bastard), and assorted others were intent on firing up a consumer boom, dashing for growth whilst maintaining lower than required interest rates. Borrowing soared and property values boomed. Whilst more sober leaders in more sober times had seen their role as 'taking away the booze before the party got too rowdy', those in power in the early 1970's unfortunately became rather intoxicated themselves and the inflation genie was out of the bottle. Rates were raised but too late. Incomes policies were attempted but failed. Retail prices rose quickly and commodity prices even quicker. Interest rates eventually reached prohibitive levels and asset values collapsed. It was no fun at all and it took an awful long time to fix. Of course there are differences today. Whilst we are seeing a surge in fuel prices, we in the West are not quite as vulnerable to Arab oil as we were then. We have also *'benefited'* from the cheap manufacture of goods overseas which has had a dampening effect on the inflation rate. Notwithstanding these factors, we see real similarities with a decade that was most unpleasant economically.

I have had many conversations over past years with people who have mocked the spectre of inflation returning. A common view has been that the increasing importation of cheaper consumer goods from the Far East would be more likely to cause a deflationary problem within Great Britain. Economists have pointed out that the falling cost of these goods would suppress inflationary growth. However, costs are rising strongly in these producing nations and the 'dampening' effect has now swung into reverse adding to the inflationary fire.

A state that extracts continually increasing amounts of cash from its populace (monies which may well have ended up as savings or investments) and spends this income (and more) on an increasingly bloated public sector will create an inflationary problem. No matter what the situation, no matter how well intentioned the aims, old style tax and spend policies cause inflation to rise. They just do. Of course the real problem with inflation is not the having of it but rather the getting rid. At some point, the Bank of England will have to increase rates in an attempt to bring things under control. However, rising rates will make things progressively difficult for mortgagees already enduring escalating housing related costs, council taxes, utility bills, etc. With payments and repayments increasing, employees will feel the obvious need to earn more and their representatives will be eyeing the inflation numbers with interest. All we will really need is Red Robbo and the Bay City Rollers to find ourselves back in the1970's.

Errors of judgment are not restricted to central banks. The startling correction in the stock market in 2008 was (according to a leading finance house) a '*25 standard deviation event*', something that is only likely to occur once every one hundred thousand years. This seems to be somewhat optimistic when one considers the relative frequency of such corrections. According to this highly respected firm's pronouncement, Methuselah himself should have only an outside chance of witnessing a

500 point drop in the FTSE 100. You don't have to understand the terminology to see the flaw.

The price of basic food stuffs is experiencing a substantial increase and we should remember that this whole business was caused by a flood of cheap money prompting investment bubbles in everything from commodities to property. Low interest rates are unlikely to prove the cure for our ills although central bankers probably feel that such rates are one of the few weapons available to them. My view is that asset markets will ultimately have to correct themselves further. There is only so much that the central bankers can do. As one commentator rather aptly put it;

'Central bankers are like toddlers driving toy cars. They think they are steering but the controls are not connected to anything.'

The causes of the sub-prime crisis have been well reported although I am surprised that even more focus has not been given to the issue of remuneration for the traders acting in this market. It is undeniable that the ability to acquire vast sums in bonuses led the financial services industry to take on unnatural amounts of risk. This phenomenon has its roots at least partly in the explosion of the hedge fund sector. As such funds tend to take circa 20% of return as opposed to the much lower commissions of the investment banks, the lure of hugely increased bonuses has tempted many of the brightest minds to join the hedge fund band wagon and one can hardly blame them for seeking such riches. The banks responded in the only way possible by amending their own payment structures in a bid to retain key staff. When you have payment plans which simply offer a slice of any and all profits then you really are inviting the kind of high risk securities trading that has brought us to the edge of ruin. After all, if you can earn several £millions per annum you only need an investment boom to last a relatively short time for you to become so wealthy that the eventual consequences of the inevitable bust become unimportant. Suffice to say, it is notable that our finest bankers have managed to bring about the nationalisation of our banks only previously advocated by the most extreme of left wingers

For every scandalous £10 million bonus paid to a city employee, the State took half. If this £10 million had been retained within the business then the State would have missed out as well as the worker. The huge profits at UK based banks meant huge taxes for the Treasury and Labour just lapped it up, even offering tax incentives to high flyers. We should therefore remember that Labour actively encouraged City excess throughout their time in office, greedily slurping up tax revenues for use on their pet projects and their mad compulsion to draft every available human soul into the public sector.

We have also become progressively more aware that at least some of the returns from hedge funds have been simply the result of gearing (using borrowed money to buy assets thereby enhancing returns when markets are rising). The same level of gearing may well have produced better returns in everyday equity funds. Gearing is good in good times but in bad times it is very, very bad and some rather big names in the hedge fund business have come a nasty cropper.

As a non-hedge fund manager I can take some spiteful delight at such failures. Some hedge funds have rather given the lie to claims that they can benefit in all market conditions. Selling short in an obviously declining market can be profitable as can the taking of long positions in a bull run. Unfortunately, when the market's direction is more uncertain then you have to choose which way to jump, not always with success. Certainly, some clever short-term strategies are beginning to look as if they are based as much on luck as on anything else. There are some very good hedge funds around but there is an awful lot of dross too. It has been said that any investment requiring the use of algebra or Greek lettering is best avoided. Having no knowledge of either, I would probably concur.

The Government is not responsible for the soaring oil price which is causing such hardship for business and motorist alike. What we are lacking however is any kind of a reserve accumulated over the years of plenty which could be used to alleviate the situation. What we have done is to spend ten years marching towards the enemy, loosing off our ammunition for the sheer hell of it, only to find our magazines empty as we finally face the foe. Taxes are rising. They will continue to rise. A recovery will be a long and very painful journey even if it is possible.

As I survey the wreckage, I still find it difficult to believe that the system has deteriorated to the degree that it has. The descent from where we were to where we are has been astonishing. All involved in the finance industry from bankers to brokers have been wearing blinkers, quite unable to imagine that such a scenario could play out. It is, after all, truly unbelievable. In a year or three someone will write the definitive history of this disaster of disasters. I shall read it with interest albeit through the gaps in my fingers.

> A feature of recent politics has been the ridiculous spectacle of politician's lacerating each other over real or perceived cuts to public spending. It is obvious to all that dramatic cuts need to be imposed on public spending and, at times, the regular tourney between party leaders has bordered on the infantile. Deeper cuts are inevitable however violently the politicos deny it. We don't have any money, one wonders quite who in the country is unaware of this.

No one should need reminding of the sheer horror of our country's finances. The deficit figures are fantastical and so huge that there is a danger we may start to ignore them, much as an individual would fret over a £10,000 loan but would dismiss from his mind a debt of £10m. It is so enormously, outrageously out of his control that he may as well shrug his burdened shoulders and pick up his golf bag. The numbers are also unlikely to be accurate as they are based on very optimistic and unsupported growth projections for the next few years. The final Labour Budget was a very political act and set a trap for the opposition in terms of their position on public spending and taxation. That said, it is plainly obvious that whatever the hue of this and future governments, taxes will need to rise substantially and an axe be taken to the public spending budget. The alternative is bankruptcy.

Should the required fiscal action not be taken, it is quite possible that the state will not be able to borrow the large amounts required, at least on reasonable terms. Such a situation would only lead to an appeal to our old chums at the IMF, who would be more than willing to administer the medicine required. Mr Osborne's figures may prove to be correct. Indeed, I hope that they are. As passionately in fact as I hope that West Ham United will win the Champions League. I am also rather chipper on the prospects of Elvis Presley touring again soon.

Even the Americans shied away from the most extreme form of quantitative easing (where a government effectively writes itself a cheque) whilst we British enthusiastically filled our boots. If taken to its logical/illogical conclusion, a persistent policy of QE would leave the world awash with valueless paper money and therefore any degree of QE puts us somewhere along that path to rack and ruin.

QE has many supporters. However, if it were true that it can be used to stimulate an economy but that the new liquidity can be withdrawn in time to avoid surging inflation then history would be littered with examples of this occurring. It would also follow that inflation could be simply controlled by adopting the 'squeezing' policy advocated by QE enthusiasts. If this were true, why on earth has any economy ever tolerated inflation when it could be so easily dealt with? The fact is that once the inflation genie is out of the bottle, it is extremely difficult to get it back in again. A policy of printing money, overspending and excessive borrowing is inflationary. It just is.

QE has caused much confusion and misunderstanding. The uneducated in financial matters would see it as simply printing money. The authorities refute this simplistic view and it is indeed a very complex matter.

There are effectively three ways of raising funds over and above taxation policy and selling off the family silver;

- **Borrowing against current taxation.**
- **Borrowing against future tax receipts.**
- **Creating further £SD, which are not covered by present or future revenues, (QE)**

The monies raised via QE were used essentially to purchase existing Gilts (originally issued with point 2 as security) to the benefit of the Treasury. The State then issued further tranches of its loan stock to replace those redeemed with their QE funds. It is very neat and a great wheeze which effectively represents a wealth transference tax from the private to the public sectors. If we are going to look at the bottom line, it *is* printing money, albeit without the cost and inconvenience of providing ink and paper. All that is needed is some old rope. There is a common view that a policy of QE may not cause too much damage just as long as some kind of rein is kept on the amounts involved. Previous instances of excessive QE have provided doubtful results. The Weimar Republic and Mugabe's Zimbabwe spring to mind.

> The simple fact is that the country's current national debt can never be repaid under any normal circumstances. It can however, be inflated away. The only problem in repaying a 50 million Mark loan in 1923 was in finding a workable wheelbarrow in which to cart the required paper. Perhaps this is the end game. If someone could possibly suggest another way of repaying trillions of pounds of debt when the country can't produce a 50 bob surplus in a good year, I would be grateful to hear it.

It is true that the finance industry is responsible for huge problems but the disastrous situation that confronts us has been effectively sponsored by the US Federal Reserve and the Bank of England amongst numerous others. There have been occasions over the past decade when the markets (if left alone) would have corrected various problems but on each of these occasions the central bankers have stepped in to keep the party going. I recall that a former Chairman of the 'Fed' once stated that his role was to remove the punchbowl whenever the party looked like getting out of hand. His modern day peers seem to believe that it is their moral duty to pour tequila slammers down the throat of every reveller they come across.

The collapse in markets saw Mr Bernard Madoff summarily dispatched by the American courts. The likely sentence was a matter of great debate both due to the defendant's age and some confusion as to the exact extent of his fraud. Personally I cannot divine an awful lot of difference between a $50Bn fraud and one for $60Bn (unless it happens to be your own spare $10Bn of course). In any case, we needn't have worried as the crestfallen fund manager was sentenced to the rather optimistic term of 150 years in the Pen. Whilst such a sentence has a deliciously brutal attraction to those of us who like our tolerance levels set at zero, it still seems a trifle over dramatic. Why not 100 years? Even a mere 50 would certainly have seen off the septuagenarian fraudster. I love American sentences; they are just so wonderfully, ridiculously and emphatically American.

The Madoff fraud teaches us that every investment must be examined and reviewed without prejudice, positive or otherwise. The collapse in the banking sector has already shown us that there can be no sacred cows. The days of holding any investment purely on name and reputation are clearly over. Please be careful.

The Gods of the Copybook Headings

As I pass through my incarnations in every age and race,
I make my proper prostrations to the Gods of the Market Place.
Peering through reverent fingers I watch them flourish and fall,
And the Gods of the Copybook Headings, I notice, outlast them all.

We were living in trees when they met us. They showed us each in turn
That Water would certainly wet us, as Fire would certainly burn:
But we found them lacking in Uplift, Vision and Breadth of Mind,
So we left them to teach the Gorillas while we followed the March of Mankind.

We moved as the Spirit listed. They never altered their pace,
Being neither cloud nor wind-borne like the Gods of the Market Place,
But they always caught up with our progress, and presently word would come
That a tribe had been wiped off its icefield, or the lights had gone out in Rome.

With the Hopes that our World is built on they were utterly out of touch,
They denied that the Moon was Stilton; they denied she was even Dutch;
They denied that Wishes were Horses; they denied that a Pig had Wings;
So we worshipped the Gods of the Market Who promised these beautiful things.

When the Cambrian measures were forming, They promised perpetual peace.
They swore, if we gave them our weapons, that the wars of the tribes would cease.
But when we disarmed They sold us and delivered us bound to our foe,
And the Gods of the Copybook Headings said: 'Stick to the Devil you know.'

On the first Feminian Sandstones we were promised the Fuller Life
(Which started by loving our neighbour and ended by loving his wife)
Till our women had no more children and the men lost reason and faith,
And the Gods of the Copybook Headings said: 'The Wages of Sin is Death.'

In the Carboniferous Epoch we were promised abundance for all,
By robbing selected Peter to pay for collective Paul;
But, though we had plenty of money, there was nothing our money could buy,
And the Gods of the Copybook Headings said: 'If you don't work you die.'

Then the Gods of the Market tumbled, and their smooth-tongued wizards withdrew
And the hearts of the meanest were humbled and began to believe it was true
That All is not Gold that Glisters, and Two and Two make Four
And the Gods of the Copybook Headings limped up to explain it once more.

As it will be in the future, it was at the birth of Man
There are only four things certain since Social Progress began.
That the Dog returns to his Vomit and the Sow returns to her Mire,
And the burnt Fool's bandaged finger goes wabbling back to the Fire;

And that after this is accomplished, and the brave new world begins
When all men are paid for existing and no man must pay for his sins,
As surely as Water will wet us, as surely as Fire will burn,
The Gods of the Copybook Headings with terror and slaughter return!

Rudyard Kipling

SEVENTEEN

RED TAPE

Any change is resisted because bureaucrats have a vested interest in the chaos in which they exist.

Richard Nixon

Over past years I have had regular occasion to apologise to my customers for the progressively intrusive data collection exercises which I have subjected them to. They are the most irritating in a long line of regulatory demands which I am not convinced will ensure the security of anything or anybody. Those inclined to cheat the system need only ignore the new regulations as they would have ignored the old ones.

Most new requirements originate in Brussels and Europhiles are at pains to emphasise that they are *regulations* and not *laws*. Unfortunately we have to obey them or we are punished, so it is difficult to discern the difference. There is a strong drive towards the elimination of risk in investment which is fine in principle but which can also be rather self defeating. A recent study indicated that contrary to common perception the compulsory use of seatbelts has not saved lives. Drivers are of course undeniably safer but therein lies the rub. We drive secured with belt, airbag and various other devices and we most certainly do feel more secure. We then tend to career around corners rather faster than we might if we had our children sloshing around in the back. This tendency has taken its toll in the form of unwitting cyclists and pedestrians.

Accordingly, the more protected investors feel, the more risk they tend to take on even if unconsciously, sometimes with disappointing results.

149

> Before the election of 2010 we understood that we could expect an incoming Tory administration to light a bonfire of the Health and Safety Regulations, beginning, we were told, in offices. I work in an office and all I have noticed is an increase in the bloody stupid rules that blight the lives of all except those who earn their livings introducing and enforcing them.

It's not that I don't appreciate the general principle of treating all clients in the same way. However, it is ridiculous to have to carry out intrusive surveys and identity checks to the same standard for someone who has been a client for 50 years, as to a swarthy Columbian with a suitcase full of used 'tenners', idly using his Tesco club card to corral lines of white powder. The folly of any 'one size fits all' policy can be confirmed by the ridiculous scenes at our airports. Wheelchair bound Englishmen have leather loafers removed from octogenarian feet and are shoved through X-ray machines whilst gaggles of foreigners sail past in garments you could hide a Lancaster bomber inside.

A year or two ago, my very tired six year old was parted from her Teddy by a concourse Kapo and watched tearfully as the previously inanimate bear was passed through the scanner muttering, 'this is bloody ridiculous' and shaking his furry head. This was in England. A far more pleasurable experience was to be had on a Christmas-time visit to Finland. Having enjoyed several days in a winter wonderland we drove off to the tiny airfield for our flight home. One lady travelled with her mother and three children. A young holiday rep assisted with the bags and waited the minute or so it took to check in. He then helped with hand luggage and buggy right up to the steps of the plane before returning through security and bidding the guards cheerio. Perhaps not quite what you would like to see at Gatwick but still an enjoyable illustration of the Finnish expectation of being detonated by a party of English families in search of Santa.

There is a serious point here. Aside from the idiocy and the hideous aggravation caused by much of the country's growing bureaucracies, the sheer enormous weight of costs should be enough to prompt some kind of rethink. Bureaucracies have mushroomed in size (as they are prone to do) and they tend to take on a life of their own with constant innovation required to justify their existence. Bureaucracy welcomes and gold plates any Whitehall or EU diktat. We have training and competence departments who again constantly innovate in order to justify and expand their influence. We need to be extremely careful here. A decade of debt fuelled prosperity has lulled us into the misconception that we are a wealthy and powerful nation that can afford all this baloney and retain a large portion of our population on welfare. We cannot.

I read recently of one authority's investigation into 'Gentlemen's clubs' headed by its 'official anti-objectification advocacy officer' (I kid you not) who operated on a very acceptable £68,000 p.a. Now I would be perfectly happy for these (I am informed) modern day Augean Stables to be closed but then I would also be more than happy to come around and dance for you for that kind of taxpayer's cash.

If you have been a customer of any finance house over the last ten years then you will have encountered the modern obsession for data collection. You may have been a customer of my firm for 50 years previously but this would not have excluded you from the requirement to prove who you are and where you live. It is patently odd that I would have written to you at your address asking for proof of who you are and where you live but the FSA is not long on irony. It was not just me of course; you would have been asked the same questions by your bank manager, accountant, solicitor and probably your paper boy. This (we are told) is an unfortunate consequence of the need to ensure that you are not the aforementioned Columbian drug baron or some fundamentalist nutter intent on bringing what is left of western civilisation to its knees.

Assuming that you are neither of these things, and that you did in fact manage to prove that you are who you say you are, then we can certainly count the exercise as a roaring success. I certainly feel safer in my bed and I expect that you do too. There is, however, the small matter of the crippling expense of it all. I have no figures for it but having watched the whole charade at first hand for a decade, I am appalled at the enormity and futility of the project. What have we achieved aside from the hideously expensive employment of hordes of money laundering officers?

How many terrorists have been caught in our net due to their inability to produce a passport that looks like a passport? And what of our Columbian drug baron friend? Has his multi-billion dollar empire been brought down by his inability to show me a gas bill that looks like a gas bill? Do we really think that such a document is beyond the wit of the world's drug cartels?

No of course not, it's absurd. The whole thing is absurd. Except in the sense that it does further the data gathering ambitions of governments a little more.

We have had ten years of growing regulation, a decade of constant regulatory innovation culminating in a complete collapse in the financial system. And what was the regulators response when their regulations failed?

We need more regulation!

No, in point of fact we do not, we may well need better regulation but that's not the same thing at all. We need it simpler and clearer. Simple and clear enough for plebs like me to be able to know what the hell the rules are this week. It was always my view of compliance that even if he was completely and blissfully unaware of the law, an honest man behaving honestly would not fall foul of the rules. If you behaved with integrity then you couldn't fail to be compliant. That was then; now, perfectly honest people walk around with the haunted look of men embroiled in love affairs with their wives sisters.

Whilst the FSA were crawling all over us checking utility bills, Merrill Lynch were busily palming off rubbish loans as quality bonds, selling things that didn't exist and generally bringing down the global financial system. This is the point; the compliance industry is just that, an industry. It employs huge numbers of people, it incurs huge costs for businesses (which are always passed on to their customers) and it prevents far more legitimate business from taking place than you would imagine. The FSA is like a bad policeman, always looking to police the policeable but unwilling and unable to deal with the devious and difficult.

For all its faults and its warts, the City of London still manages to provide something around 20% of this country's GDP. It is invaluable to the nation's treasury and employs millions of people either directly or indirectly. It is a goose that lays golden eggs. It can be an unruly goose at times but killing it will only result in a dead goose and no eggs. I would prefer for the City to provide a much smaller proportion of our wealth but only if we have managed to rebuild other industries and not because the City has been castrated. Without the finance industry our country would immediately collapse under the weight of its burdens and the city's politically inspired enemies should be vehemently opposed.

EIGHTEEN

HALF A CROWN

*I know I have but the body of a weak and feeble woman, but I have the heart of a
king, and of a king of England, too, and think foul scorn that Parma or Spain, or
any prince of Europe should dare to invade the borders of my realm; to which, rather
than any dishonour should grow by me, I myself will take up arms, I myself will be
your general, judge, and rewarder of every one of your virtues in the field.*

Elisabeth I

Sadly, we would be foolish to expect anything similar to the above from
Elisabeth II. I am certainly a monarchist at heart but am sorely
disappointed with the Windsors and sadly, with the Monarch herself.
Like most Englishmen, I am quite fond of her and I accept that she does
a superb job; it's just that she does the wrong one.

Supposedly, the Queen has little constitutional power. This is not
altogether true. Take (for example) the Lisbon Treaty (EU Constitution
Bill) and the disgusting, lick spittle and underhand way in which it was
ratified in this country. Everyone understood that there was a manifesto
pledge to hold a referendum on the constitution question. Everyone
understood that the Lisbon Treaty represented the Constitution Bill. It
may have been worded a little differently and perhaps printed in a
different font but every honest man acknowledged that the two
documents were essentially one and the same. Refusing a referendum
and signing the treaty behind closed doors was therefore deceitful,
dishonest and spat in the face of the democratic ideal.

Brown is quite happy with this but is our Queen equally content? The patriot in me likes to think that she is not, so why has she acquiesced in this deceit and indeed in so many others over the years?

Our Sovereign signed a document that transferred sovereignty from herself and her people to a foreign power without the consent, and against the clear wish of her people. I am not interested in the constitutional niceties of this kind of thing.

The Queen shouldn't have signed that piece of paper.

If her refusal to do so provoked a constitutional crisis then all well and good, it was after all a constitutional issue. Actually, public opinion would have been very much in her corner and it would have been a good way to round off her 50 odd years of waving, smiling and smashing Champagne into ships while her governments sold us down the river.

She could even have signed the bloody thing a bit later, after her cheating First Lord had been rebuked for his dishonesty. She should certainly have signed later still if her subjects had given their approval for her to do so. The Crown is supposed to be the people's defence and champion against tyranny and treachery, our bulwark against those who would sell us out for short term political gain. The Queen is supposed to be on our side, permanently and passionately. If she does not or will not defend our rights then save from cutting ribbons there is no purpose to her existence. If she is to collude in and condone the machinations of politicians then she is just a little old lady in a big house and of no material use to her people whatsoever.

I want my Sovereign to appear in my defence and not on a tea towel. She is supposed to be the Queen of England after all, the Queen of the English, defender of the faith and protector of the people's rights. Can she really be happy with what has become of us, or is she simply willing to comply with her Government's dishonesty so that her grandson can still be driven from his wedding in a golden coach?

I don't give two hoots for her beloved Commonwealth which seems to operate as a mechanism by which our former colonies can humiliate and insult us whilst emptying our pockets. The colonies have their independence, let them enjoy and make full use of it. The Germans don't seem to have need of such a thing and they seem to be jogging along reasonably well. Does Norway have a commonwealth? Does Japan? Does Switzerland?

The thing is a nonsense whose only real purpose seems to be to allow us a sniff of a medal in track and field at those games that nobody watches on the television. Do the Indians see the Commonwealth as anything other than an occasionally useful vehicle through which they can acquire some satisfaction or another? The Commonwealth exists as a conduit through which Britain can prostrate and humiliate herself before her former vassals, in public and in perpetuity. We should have no more of this weak kneed idiocy and must look to form new ties of friendship and commerce with the Commonwealth nations like grown-ups.

NINETEEN

OPTIONS AND POSSIBILITIES

Wake up England!

George V

What is required is a genuine movement of the right, not some extremist lunacy but not the comfortable, 'I'm all right in the shires Jack' nonsense of the Tory party either.

- We need a party that will compel the unwilling to work but also ensure that not only is there work for them to do but that it is rewarding enough to change the mindset of the unproductive.
- We need a party that will not permit people to evade their responsibilities at our expense.
- We need a party that will enforce the law rigorously but that will respect the individual's right to go about his lawful business unmolested by the state.
- We need a party that will pursue the wicked and deal with them justly and firmly on behalf of the public.
- We need a party that will value its own people and that will ensure their education, training and gainful employment.
- We need a party that will do all that is required to ensure that we have strong defences but consider them for use only sparingly, in our interests and not used as some convenient toy whenever something goes wrong in the world.

- We need a party that will stop the flood of cheap foreign labour that so undermines the English working man and woman.

- We need a party that is open to other cultures but that favours and protects our own.

- We need a party that will forge the strongest and friendliest links with other nations but that will refrain from attempting to merge with them or submit ourselves to them.

- We need a party that will tackle the powerful vested interests that infect our public services and ensure that these services exist to serve the public and not those who work within them.

- We need a party that will, in its first act of government, state clearly the permanent sovereignty of the Westminster Parliament.

- We need a party that readily recognises that our people and our culture are worth preserving and will commit to do all in its power to achieve this end.

Yes but! Yes but! Well my friend there is always a yesbut, a reason or an excuse as to why these things are only ever promised and never achieved. Such promises are only made by politicians when safe in the knowledge that a yesbut will turn up to save them from having to deliver. Our political class is a cabal, a monopoly operating within a system that is designed to ensure its own survival. We may vote red or blue or even yellow but the individuals we are actually electing are generally drawn from the same stock and are, in any case, put before us in a fait accompli. Our democracy is a feeble joke compared with what could have been achieved. A thousand years ago, the Anglo Saxons used to elect their Kings and yet we don't even get to choose which set of chinless wonders are put before us at election time.

- Do you not think that our more 'off with the fairies' judges might reconsider releasing rapists on bail if they thought that the public might bring them to heel when it was time for their re-election.
- Do you not think that Chief Constables might be a little less PC and a little more PC Plod if they needed the public's support?
- What if the people oppose immigration? Then it should stop.
- What if they favour the death penalty? Then they should have it.
- What if they wish to be favoured over other nations and peoples? Then they should be so favoured.

Admittedly this is populist stuff but what of it? Why shouldn't a government enact policies that are popular with the people that elect it? Why can't a government be popular and not despised?

So you may see that I am in favour of democracy but only of that elusive kind which results in the people actually getting what they want, rather than what is thought good for them by an authoritarian class that has failed miserably and consistently in everything but its own continuation.

Granted, you may think that I am a dreamer or even an extremist; I can accept that, but just take a look at what *you* have accepted over the past seventy years or so.

- The loss of Empire
- The destruction of our towns and cities in an unnecessary and unwinnable war.

- The deaths and maiming of hundreds of thousands of young men torn from their homes to fight this war.
- The deaths and maiming of thousands of civilians in bombing campaigns.
- The deaths and maiming of countless millions of people belonging to other nations.
- The bankruptcy and debt incurred by a war we could never truly win.
- The termination of millions of unborn children
- The importation of millions of foreigners to compete with our own working class.
- The liberalisation of our justice system to the point where the guilty go free and the innocent are disregarded.
- The refusal of our leaders to deal effectively with a drug culture that accounts for the majority of recorded crimes and which blights the lives of every section of British society.
- The destruction of the manufacturing industry which had brought us wealth, dignity for our workers and respect in the world.
- The perpetuation of a political system and class that cares little, if at all, for the people it supposedly represents.
- Having to wash out your empty baked bean tins to comply with the green mafia.

James Goldsmith had a sound idea before the 1997 election. Why not ask the public what they would like to do about Europe in a referendum? Thus was born the Referendum Party. Goldsmith's subsequent death was a great pity because he showed every sign of taking the project to its logical conclusion. Form a government and then ask the people what they would like to see happen on the major issues of the day. Then give them what they asked for. The prospect was, and is, horrific to the political classes and this tells you all you need to know about them.

Wouldn't it be nice if someone else would come along to take up the baton? Wouldn't it be nice for us to actually decide our own destiny? We could eschew party politics for a short while and let the people decide the major issues of the day. Perhaps we could have polls on the likes of the following;

- **Do you wish to re-instate the death penalty for those who would murder children?**
- **Do you wish to leave the European Union?**
- **Do you wish to end immigration into the UK?**
- **Do you wish to directly elect your senior police chiefs and judiciary?**

That's just for starters. I suspect that once people got the taste for some real democracy then they may even come to enjoy it.

MPs would still be in the privileged position of being able to influence the electorate far more than any layman opposing them. Indeed, they have had this privilege all through the post war period and are still not confident of having indoctrinated the public to their points of view. Perhaps you might imagine that this would have had some impact on their own certainties? Not a bit of it and do you know why? It's because they consider you to be an ignorant peasant who couldn't possibly have a better notion of right and wrong than they do, that's why.

Many of our current MP's may not feel capable of continuing if affirmative answers were given to these questions. They may not feel that they could continue to serve if they are compelled to carry out the people's wishes. They may need to stand down. That would be noble, admirable and very, very welcome.

TWENTY

INDEPENDENCES OR UNIONS

Desperate affairs require desperate measures.

Admiral Horatio Nelson

There are urgent conversations to be had concerning the tangled weave of our agreements and alliances and whether we should be looking to untangle the web somewhat. There is a case to be made for our withdrawal from many of the unions that entangle us and we should at least contemplate our positions with regard to;

- **The Commonwealth**
- **NATO**
- **The United Nations**
- **The European Union**
- **The UN Convention on refugees (asylum).**
- **The United Kingdom**

To start with, we should have a referendum on English independence as well as similar polls in all the other home nations. Let us see if we wish for our British union to continue before we go any further. If all four countries wish to continue then public approval of the union would quite likely clear the air a little. If they do not, then we should part. Whatever the outcome, it should be respected with no further poll for at least ten years. Countries opting out could always re-apply for membership at some future point should they wish to do so and, of course, with the agreement of the other member nations.

An English vote for independence would offer all manner of interesting opportunities. It is the United Kingdom that is member of and signatory to all of the restrictive bodies and agreements that are the bain of our lives and that seem to continually bring trouble to our door. The United Kingdom is the member of NATO, of the Commonwealth and of the European Union. Not England. It is a murky old business and the 'constitutional experts' will wring their hands but I suspect that an English vote to secede from the United Kingdom would be the one mighty bound that would set us free from a hundred years of political fix-ups and back room betrayals.

If there is some legal technicality that would prevent such a break then I recommend that we follow the French model and simply ignore it.

We may choose to negotiate English re-entry into these supra-national bodies but would there be much in the way of enthusiasm to do so? How many of us would vote to rejoin the Commonwealth as its whipping boy? How many would clamour to resign the convention on asylum? How many would be happy to again throw in our lot with the EU, certainly on anything like the present arrangements and terms?

Would we lose influence? Certainly, who cares? We are not a global power so why continue the pretence that we are? Other nations do not feel the need to do so, so why do we continue to overstretch and endanger ourselves?

The EU is our biggest market but one on which we have always made a hefty loss so it is unlikely that our friends on the continent would send us to Coventry.

A military independence would undoubtedly diminish our role in the 'shoot 'em up' stakes and so we would not be able to have quite so many wars, not necessarily a bad thing you might agree.

I am not advocating disengagement from the world, far from it. I *am* advocating disengagement from many of the worlds alliances in order that we may assess the damage caused by them, regroup and re-launch ourselves on the world stage as a vibrant, respectful (of others *and* ourselves) nation of peaceful tradesmen. If we truly believe that we cannot have our independence *and* our daily bread then we must consider ourselves inferior to those peoples who do. If this is the case then we may as well close up the shop now and let the Tower Hamlets Taliban run things.

- **If our population shrinks, so what?**
- **If our GDP figures fall and we decline in those little league tables we see in the newspapers, so what?**

I happen to think that we would not be losing quite so many of our sons and daughters if the country was managed better, if our people felt valued and rewarded for their efforts and loyalties, if England was seen as a place where enterprise and hard work were rewarded with something other than red tape and ridiculous levels of taxation. Perhaps if national pride was encouraged, *genuinely* encouraged and citizenship of our nation was seen as a great and valuable prize, not something received automatically through the post or handed out like lollipops in Dover in exchange for a lie and a promise, then perhaps our people would find the reserves of energy to respond.

Do we really feel that all those English people, those *millions* of English people have left this country because of the weather? This is, I would suggest, extremely unlikely. They leave for many reasons, all of which share one simple, underlying theme; they do not wish to stay *here* anymore.

Whether it is the high taxes, the hypocrisy or the scary demographics and the general abuse that propels them overseas, the fact is that England is losing millions of its own best people just as she did during Empire. Should we attempt to improve things so that more of our people wish to stay with us or should we simply replace them with whatever is available from abroad?

Even if were true that our country is improved by new blood, I still can't see how the English can welcome this. We are what we are. We should succeed or fail, suffer or prosper and live or die on our own exertions.

We would all quite like our offspring to excel in their working lives. If it were proved that the Japanese were intellectually superior to us, maybe we could ensure the success of our progeny by forcing our mediocre children to leave home and getting in some really clever kids from Tokyo? The performance of our children would be improved would it not?

Does it not therefore make sense to run down the English numbers and replace them with Japanese? As soon as all the thick Englishmen were gone our new England would be a far better place.

Only they wouldn't be our children.

And it wouldn't be England.

If we believe that we need all those alliances and unions then we are effectively concluding that we are incapable of survival alone. If we really and truly believe this, then it is really and truly all over for us.

Quite how England has become so cowed and timid is a great mystery to me. Perhaps it is as it is for a great prize fighter whose long career ends when he simply cannot bear the thought of another blow.

TWENTY ONE

CAPTEN, ART THA SLEEPIN' THERE BELOW?

There must be a beginning of any great matter, but the continuing unto the end until it be thoroughly finished yields the true glory.

Sir Francis Drake

Much of what I have written may be seen as insensitive or outdated by some, a relic perhaps of another age. I don't care about that; we have all beaten around the bush for far too long.. Should this little book gain any attention then it will be subjected to forensic ridicule and my character will be assassinated. I don't care about that either. It is not even that the things I have written needed to be written, they have been said in every pub, gentlemen's and working men's club in England for a very long time. It is just that I needed to say them, to get them down on paper, for my own sanity.

I have not looked to deliberately offend anyone for their birth or origin. A man should only be accountable for his actions and not the lottery of his birth. The only genuine loathing I feel is directed at those of our own people who have systemically sold us out and have got away with it. I do regret the sloth of the English, we are undoubtedly intellectually lazy. It is said that we may only be pushed so far before our spirits harden and we 'turn' and fight like lions. I think that, actually, our empire, our wars and our defeatism have sapped our strength to such a low point that there is probably no real prospect of recovery.

I do so hope that this is not true but I fear greatly that it is. It is a depressing thought and not a very jolly way to end my little missive. Perhaps one day Drake will indeed return. I occasionally peer out to sea in wistful hope that he may.

Yours ever,

Adam.

EPILOGUE

Just days from this book going to press, the English reaped the harvest of their post war insanity. Several summer days of uncontrolled anarchy may finally have woken our people to the consequences of their indifference and to the nightmare future which we have built for ourselves. We have been confronted (reluctantly) with the reality of life in our cities, a reality which is terrifying to acknowledge but which it would be suicidal to ignore. The numbers of rioters was small relative to the population as a whole but this does tend to re-illustrate a point made earlier in this book. A weak state and people cannot cope with a determined minority (of any group) hell-bent on destruction and disorder. This is not to advocate some savage police state or a Regular Army presence in our cities but this is what awaits us if we continue to tolerate the destructive ultra-liberal mentality that has brought us to this point and which will take us to our eventual demise.

Liberalism will lead us to death or the Gestapo.

It is perhaps too late to address the situation without repression but I hope that we can raise the strength for one last attempt at saving ourselves.

Many of our errors have contributed to the events of August 2011. We have an ill disciplined and indulgent education system that respects all pupil rights except that to have a structured, ordered and effective education. We have also reaped the rewards of an immigration system which has demanded neither integration nor participation in English society. Many of the rioters were 'white British' but very few I suspect have been raised into 'white British' culture and society.

When three young Asian men were murdered by a black man in Birmingham, there were fears of race war erupting in our second city and around the country. The media has claimed the avoidance of such a conflict as evidence that our multi-cultural society truly works. However, in the same breath the press attributed the averting of racial conflict to the dignity of the father of one of the victims. Indeed, this gentleman showed huge courage and dignity in incredibly difficult circumstances. His calming words were largely responsible for avoiding a meltdown in his city and perhaps nationwide. A racial conflict of real proportions was avoided because this one man called for peace.

But what if he hadn't? What if his instinct had been for retribution and revenge? If he had not pleaded with the young men of his community to stay home, we could reasonably have expected to have had a blood bath on our hands. What happens the next time the son of one 'community' is murdered by the son of another? It would seem inevitable that at some point an interracial murder will provoke the war that many of us dread but confidently expect.

It is all incredibly sad but there is no longer any point in pretending that we live in a cohesive society. We either give up now or we somehow find the resolve to deal with our fractured nation. Unfortunately, it is patently obvious that the vast bulk of our political class are incapable of truly governing outside of Dorset or Devon. They cannot understand that the diverse and liberated nation they have built is, in fact, divided and forever on the cusp of anarchy and collapse. We have had a taste of the future. Without a radical change in our mindset, an eventual collapse of our society is as sure as night follows day. Salvation for the English is a huge challenge but we can hope that someone or something will emerge to salvage what can be salvaged from the havoc wreaked by our post war liberal delusion.

Capten, art tha sleepin' there below?

174

And did those feet in ancient time
Walk upon England's mountains green?
And was the Holy Lamb of God
On England's pleasant pastures seen?
And did the Countenance divine
Shine forth upon those clouded hills?
And was Jerusalem builded here,
Among those dark satanic mills?

Bring me my bow of burning gold,
Bring me my arrows of desire;
Bring me my spear! O, clouds unfold!
Bring me my chariot of fire!
I will not cease from mental fight,
Nor shall my sword sleep in my hand
Till we have built Jerusalem
In England's green and pleasant land.

William Blake

Each of you, for himself, by himself and on his own responsibility, must speak. And it is a solemn and weighty responsibility, and not lightly to be flung aside at the bullying of pulpit, press, government, or the empty catchphrases of politicians. Each must for himself alone decide what is right and what is wrong, and which course is patriotic and which isn't. You cannot shirk this and be a man. To decide against your convictions is to be an unqualified and inexcusable traitor, both to yourself and to your country, let man label you as they may. If you alone of all the nation shall decide one way, and that way be the right way according to your convictions of the right, you have done your duty by yourself and by your country- hold up your head! You have nothing to be ashamed of.

Mark Twain

If all things are always the same, it is because they are always heroic. If all things are always the same, it is because they are always new. To each man one soul only is given, to each soul only is given a little power, the power at some moments to outgrow and swallow up the stars. If age after age that power comes upon men, whatever gives it to them is great. Whatever makes men feel old is mean-an empire or a skin-flint shop. Whatever makes men feel young is great, a great war or a love story. And in the darkest of the books of God there is written a truth which is also a riddle. It is the old things that startle and intoxicate. It is the old things that are young. There is no sceptic who does not feel that many have doubted before. There is no rich and fickle man who does not feel upon his neck the vast weight of the universe. But we who do the old things are fed by nature with a perpetual infancy. No man who is in love thinks that anyone has been in love before. No woman who has a child thinks that there have been such things as children. No people that fight for their own city are haunted with the burden of broken empires.

Yes, O dark voice, the world is always the same, for it is always unexpected.

G K Chesterton

A nation can survive its fools, and even the ambitious. But it cannot survive treason from within. An enemy at the gates is less formidable, for he is known and carries his banner openly. But the traitor moves amongst those within the gate freely, his sly whispers rustling through all the alleys, heard in the very halls of government itself. For the traitor appears not a traitor; he speaks in accents familiar to his victims, and he wears their face and their arguments, he appeals to the baseness that lies deep in the hearts of all men. He rots the soul of a nation, he works secretly and unknown in the night to undermine the pillars of the city, he infects the body politic so that it can no longer resist. A murderer is less to fear.

Cicero

Tyranny, like hell, is not easily conquered; yet we have this consolation with us, that the harder the conflict, the more glorious the triumph.

Society in every state is a blessing, but government, even in its best state is but a necessary evil; in its worst state an intolerable one.

A long habit of not thinking a thing wrong gives it a superficial appearance of being right.

We are not moved by the gloomy smile of a worthless king, but by the ardent glow of generous patriotism. We fight not to enslave, but to set a country free, and to make room upon the earth for honest men to live in. In such a case we are sure that we are right; and we leave to you the despairing reflection of being the tool of a miserable tyrant.

Thomas Paine

The democracy will cease to exist when you take away from those who are willing to work and give to those who would not.

Thomas Jefferson

Remember, democracy never lasts long. It soon wastes, exhausts, and murders itself. There never was a democracy yet that did not commit suicide.

John Adams

A government big enough to give you everything you want is big enough to take everything you have.

Barry Goldwater

The best way to destroy the capitalist system is to debase the currency.

Lenin

American politicians do anything for money... English politicians take the money and won't do anything .

Stephen Leacock

Today Americans would be outraged if UN troops entered Los Angeles to restore order; tomorrow they will be grateful! This is especially true if they were told there was an outside threat from beyond, whether real or promulgated, that threatened our very existence. It is then that all peoples of the world will pledge with world leaders to deliver them from this evil. The one thing every man fears is the unknown. When presented with these scenarios, individual rights will be willingly relinquished for the guarantee of their well being granted to them by their world government.

Henry Kissinger-*in an address to a Bilderberg group meeting in 1992*

But we are the people of England; and we have not spoken yet. Smile at us, pay us, pass us by. But never forget.

G K Chesterton

He that wishes to see his country robbed of its rights can not be a patriot.

Samuel Johnson

We are with Europe, but not of it. We are linked, but not combined. We are interested and associated, but not absorbed. And Should European statesman address us in the words which were used of old – 'Shall I speak for thee to the King or the Lord of the Host?' – we should reply with the words of the Shunamite woman: Nay sir, for we dwell among our own people.

Sir Winston Churchill

At the oval and in Trafalgar Square, there was only one flag, and it was England's. There was only one song, Blake's. If you can't be a nation until you have your own national anthem, this is a hurdle the English have now cleared. So England stirs, with implications beyond the borders of the green and pleasant land, perhaps most importantly for Scotland. That's fitting, because Scotland has unwittingly played a part in the stirring. A sense of fairness is embedded deep in the English soul … the fairness of not jumping the queue, of tutting disapprovingly of those who do. We don't mind waiting, you see, just as long as everybody is made to wait the same way. So the constitutional imbalance of Scotland's parliament and Wales's assembly plays an important part in the English story. Most English people remain ignorant of the details of devolution, and of the arguments over the Barnett formula, Scotland's oil and the rest. But since 1999 there has been a vague, nagging feeling that, politically, the Celts have jumped the queue.

James Kirkup

I love my country, and trust that I shall not be found wanting when the day comes to act. That dear old country – I wonder if a fraction of its inhabitants appreciate its worth, or does it require a probation of long absences to show one that that little island is the best, the very best place on God's earth.

HR Bowers

Yes, England - the country that dare not speak its name. In England we have this dreadful inhibition about talking about ourselves. England is a historic country which has shaped the world we are in. It is arguably the very origins of modernity. That is something we should celebrate, not be ashamed of.

David Starkey

Something stirs deep in the blood of the English. The whole notion (of devolution) stimulates, and offends their atavistic sense of fair play and decency...if there is writing on Hadrian's Wall it reads that the English should leave Scotland to its own devices... the new English Nation that must be forged must... be one as free as possible from the meaningless trappings of sentiment. The new English will be first and foremost a mercantile people, whose relations with the world are those primarily of a business partner...the English have every reason to believe that this can be a prosperous and constructive future in which England is a force for good, moderation and sanity, and in which the English state serves first and foremost the interests of the English people.

Simon Heffer

Truth is like the sun. You can shut it out for a time, but it ain't goin' away.

Elvis Presley

England expects that every man will do his duty.

Admiral Horatio Nelson

There is no such nationality as English.

John Prescott.

I hope that you have taken something from this book. My one wish for it is that it may make some small contribution to a debate which has been suppressed and which urgently needs to take place. I would welcome any comments or indeed criticisms that you may have and these can be posted on the WFD website or sent to the Post Office box detailed below. Thank you for reading.

Adam Wayne

'Waiting for Drake' is available from Amazon, eBay or through any major bookseller. Copies can also be purchased from the WFD website.

WFD
PO Box No 657
Rochester
Kent
ME1 9HT

www.waitingfordrake.com